Who Cares

about the

MISSIONARY ?

by

Marjorie A. Collins

Fourth printing published by:

Don Wardell —
Box 325
WINONA LAKE, Ind. 46590

Consideration is being given to a revision of this book for the next printing. Comments and suggestions would be appreciated.

ISBN: 0-8024-9496-X

First Printing	1974
Second Printing	1975
Third Printing	1978
Fourth Printing	1982

Printed in the United States of America

To
my dear friend,
Eleanor Lasier Rowe,
who not only believes in,
but is an example of the truth,
"Living is giving"

CONTENTS

FOREWORD

There is something special about a missionary. He not only hears, he *does!* He has listened to the voice of God's Holy Spirit, he has wrestled with the conviction placed upon him, he has trained, he has worked hard, he has arranged thousands of details, and he finally has arrived upon his field of activity. Periodically, he comes home. How can we best help him in this all important task of going into all the world with the gospel?

Certainly, we must pray. William Carey said, "If a temple is raised for God in the heathen world, it will not be by might, nor by power, nor by the authority of the magistrate, or the eloquence of the orator, but by my Spirit saith the Lord of Hosts. Therefore, we must seek His blessing upon our effort." You will find an excellent chapter in this book on the place and need of prayer in missionary endeavor.

But, in addition to this, we are clearly challenged in this volume to a whole series of extremely practical ways in which we may enhance our support of these servants of the Lord.

The material in this manual will help you and your church become even better and more effective in your support and encouragement of your missionaries. It contains an inclusive and highly practical listing of ways and means by which we all can more fully cooperate in the response to the Great Commission to go into all the world and preach the gospel. Park Street Church, here in Boston, has long been committed to the task and joy of missions. We have put into practice some of the things that are presented here, and we intend

to make this volume available to our board of missions in
order that we might more effectively fulfill our role in the
Lord's work.

Everyone can learn from these chapters. The suggestions
go all the way from *abandonment* (keep in touch with your
missionary) to *zenana* (you may have to look this one up, but
it has to do with restricting missionaries to certain audiences).
Thus, we go from A to Z, and every chapter will give new
hints and suggestions for our common task.

Third John 8 speaks of our being "fellow-helpers to the
truth." *The Living Bible* paraphrases this, "So we ourselves
should take care of them in order that we may become partners with them in the Lord's work." "Partners in the Lord's
work"—this indeed ought to be our goal. This book will
help us along the way toward achieving that goal.

PAUL E. TOMS
Pastor

PREFACE

When our Lord had an important message to give to His people, He usually used short words. His commands were simple and direct: "Come, see, hear, do, believe, be, pray, watch, go." There was no begging, no excess wordage, no room for alternatives, just the straightforward message of a loving and longing heart.

Why is it so easy for us to obey in some things and be so disobedient in others? Why is it easier to do than to be? Why are we so willing to hear but so reticent to believe? Why did we come to Jesus if we are not prepared to go for Him?

The familiar Matthew 11:28 invites us into a personal fellowship with our Saviour. He offers to carry His part of the load, and He pledges to meet our needs. "Come unto me, all ye that labour and are heavy laden, and I will give you rest." Who of us would not respond to one who not only promises but is able to perform? There was something in it for us. With very little effort, we came, and by all the power of the wisdom of God, Jesus fulfilled His commitment to us.

Now you have been brought into a new, vital, and realistic relationship with God through the Lord Jesus Christ. Even so, among those who are called Christians because they are followers of Christ, a great number close their ears to the Lord's "Go." Having experienced salvation themselves, they settle back in contentment, enjoying the rest He bestows, satisfied that heaven will someday be their destiny.

Yet, the command of the Lord in Mark 16:15 ("Go ye into all the world, and preach the gospel to every creature") is as

clear as His invitation to be accepted by God through faith in
Jesus Christ (Jn 3:36). Some will say, "But that command
of Jesus was given to His disciples. *They* were to go and
preach, and teach, and disciple, and be witnesses."

Even if we were to grant that such an interpretation is possible and plausible (and I do not), we would still be faced
with the challenge of the Lord's "Go."

What do you do with 1 Corinthians 15:58? "Therefore, my
beloved brethren, be ye stedfast, unmoveable, always abound-
ing in the work of the Lord, forasmuch as ye know that your
labour is not in vain in the Lord."

And what of Colossians 3:16? "Let the word of Christ
dwell in you richly in all wisdom; teaching and admonishing
one another in psalms and hymns and spiritual songs." Or
chapter 4, verse 5? "Walk in wisdom toward them that are
without, redeeming the time." Or 2 Timothy 2:2? "The
things that thou hast heard of me among many witnesses, the
same commit thou to faithful men, who shall be able to
teach others also."

There is no evidence in the Word of God that salvation is
to be kept only to oneself. There is a flood of evidence that
the knowledge of God is to be shared with others. There is
no room for a "saved and safe attitude." The message of the
gospel is not only a once-for-all decision which gives us a
ticket to heaven and the security of seeing saved loved ones
again after death; the gospel is for life, not only for after death.
It is not only past and future, but indeed, is decidedly present. It is not just for the individual; it is for the world. There
are no racial, political, ethnic, or economic restrictions attached to the good news of God's provision for man's need.
"There is no respect of persons with God" (Ro 2:11).

God's love extends beyond the confines of our own personal
experience. We read, "The field is *the world*" (Mt 13:38);
"For God so loved *the world* (Jn 3:16); *"Other sheep* I have"
(Jn 10:16).

For most of you, missions are an accepted form and norm of Christian living. Although you may not have been called to what is often termed "full-time missionary service," you serve as the opportunity arises; you believe that the church exists for missions, and you are attempting to further the gospel to the ends of the earth by your own involvement, as God directs.

This book is written for you who want to have an active part in getting the gospel to every creature, you who are concerned and want to be involved. You did not feel the call of God upon your own life for home or foreign missionary service, but in order to become a greater part of God's program, you have made a decision to support a missionary or missionaries.

This book is not written to tell you how to set up a missions committee in your church. It will not be merely a thesis on the importance of missionary endeavor. It will not provide all the answers to all your questions, for many of these answers can be found in other books and publications. It will not give you the details of how to have a successful missionary conference. But it is my hope that it will begin to answer these two questions: Of what does missionary support consist? and How can I become more involved in missions?

1

PRAYER

"Pray for us."

The missionary speaker has concluded the service. He may have been well dressed or shabby; he may have been involved in home missions or foreign service; he may have been a good speaker or a poor one; he may have held special interest for you or not much at all; he may have embellished his presentation with a film or slides, or perhaps he merely spoke of his field and ministry; he could have come from an urban situation, or from a little-heard-of tribe down country; you may have known him for years, or this may have been your first encounter; he might have been single or married; he could have been serving with a faith mission board or a denominational one; he may have served one term or six; he might have been a native of your area, or a stranger; he may have told of great revivals or barren efforts; he may have given an optimistic or pessimistic report; he may have mentioned that the doors to his field may close soon, or he could have told of wide open doors of opportunity with few, if any, restrictions placed on the servants of God; he may work among Moslems or Hindus, atheists or devil-worshipers, animists or Taoists, Buddhists or Zoroastrians; he may work in an isolated area, or on a station with one hundred other missionaries; he could be a pilot, doctor, electrician, teacher, nurse, Christian education expert, writer, photographer, engineer, technician, communications major, evangelist, preacher, house parent, officer manager, field director, secretary, children's worker,

15

builder, mechanic, or one of many other professionals; he
might be an advisor, or he might be responsible for an entire
area of ministry; he could be rich or poor, happy or disappointed, discouraged or defeated, successful or frustrated; he
might get along with his co-workers, or there may be serious
tensions present; he might speak his new language like a national, or he may be poor in communication; he may have ad-
justed well to the new climate, culture, and people, or he may
have found it extremely difficult; he may be in good health or
poor physical condition. No matter the conditions, your missionary will cry out to you for prayer help.

Prayer is that powerful communication line connecting
man to God—the means of praise, intercession, request—
whereby we are able to move the mountains and obstacles
which lie in the way of fulfilling the will of God. It is not
a one-way transmitter, for our words do not fall on deaf ears.
God hears. God answers.

One of our new communications satellites operates on a
millionth of a millionth watt of power. The power is in the
receiver, not in the transmitter. Thus it is with prayer. As
human beings, we do not have the power to fulfill our prayer
requests. But the Lord Jesus said, "If ye have faith as a
grain of mustard seed . . . nothing shall be impossible unto
you" (Mt 17:20). "With men it is impossible, but not with
God: for with God all things are possible" (Mk 10:27).

The Word of God exhorts us to do what our missionaries
request of us. Samuel understood that a lack of prayerful
concern was sin in his life, and thus he stated, "Moreover as
for me, God forbid that I should sin against the LORD in ceasing to pray for you" (1 Sa 12:23). David, although busy, involved, in fear for his life, was able to say, "Evening, and
morning, and at noon, will I pray, and cry aloud" (Ps 55:17).
Jesus not only practiced prayer Himself, but He exhorted His
followers to do so. "Men ought always to pray, and not to
faint" (Lk 18:1). Paul's instruction to Timothy admonished,

"I will therefore that men pray every where, lifting up holy hands, without wrath and doubting" (1 Ti 2:8). And to encourage us, James states, "Pray one for another . . . The effectual fervent prayer of a righteous man availeth much" (Ja 5:16).

Prayer ought to be a natural communion with the Lover of our souls. "When the burdens press and the cares distress," there is a quiet place of fellowship and sharing within the throne room of our God. No appointment is necessary. Jesus assures us, "Ask, and it shall be given you; seek, and ye shall find; knock, and it shall be opened unto you" (Mt 7:7). He also said, "Whatsoever ye shall ask the Father in my name, he will give it you. Hitherto have ye asked nothing in my name: ask, and ye shall receive, that your joy may be full" (Jn 16:23-24).

We are to cast our cares upon Him (1 Pe 5:7). I heard a preacher paraphrase this verse to read, "Put your care in His heart and He'll put His peace in yours." All our cares and concerns should be shared with him. Again Paul says in Philippians 4:6, "Be careful for nothing; but in every thing by prayer and supplication with thanksgiving let your requests be made known unto God." The next verse tells us that in so doing, we obtain the peace of God.

Prayer is a privilege; it is an open gateway to the fullness and power of God which are waiting to be released on behalf of ourselves and others; it is free access to the presence of God; it is the highest and holiest fellowship given to man.

Now, your missionary comes to you and says, "Pray for us." Your emotions may be stirred in that instant. You may write your name on a piece of paper saying you will fulfill that vital commitment. You may raise your hand to indicate this support. You may make a quiet resolve in your heart to remember this servant daily before the Lord. As you walk through the church doors to the broad spectrum of the world's needs beyond, you may take the missionary's hand and say, "We'll be praying for you."

But what happens to your best intentions? The following week, a close friend becomes seriously ill and is taken to the hospital. A co-worker at the office dies. Your children are involved in school programs and athletic events. Meanwhile other speakers visit the church in rapid succession. You become involved in the events taking place around you, and soon that promise to pray becomes relegated to one of those unused cell blocks of the brain—not entirely forgotten, but certainly not utilized.

The story is told of a young missionary who went off to the Far East. His home church supported him financially and promised to pray for him. He had kept them informed of his activities through letters and tapes, but unknown to him, only the chairman of the missions committee ever read or listened to them. He had a difficult time learning the language. There was great opposition from the government and non-Christian forces in his area. Then, at only twenty-six years of age, his wife contracted blackwater fever. She lived only a short time, leaving him with three young children.

He finished his first term of service, anticipating that day when he would return to his home church, to be accepted and comforted by those who loved and cared, those who had been interested enough to send him out. When the time finally came, he walked into the midweek prayer service without prior announcement. He saw only strangers, and since he had arrived just on time for the service to start, he sat in one of the back pews. No one welcomed him. He smiled at the pastor, but there was no response. The prayer period was held. There was concern for the Sunday school picnic, the new building program, the women's coming trip to a regional conference. There was no mention of missionaries, no pleading for souls, no apparent concern for a lost and dying humanity beyond the confines of their little group.

Following the service, the brokenhearted missionary stood at the back of the church. Most people did not recognize him. The few who did merely exchanged a hurried "Hello. How are you?" As the pastor finally approached him, the missionary cried out, "Now I understand. This is the reason."

"What do you mean?" questioned the pastor.

"Those years on the field. The difficulties. The pain. The lack of results. This is the reason." He went on to confess his supreme disappointment that he had been forgotten, but most of all that he had not been prayed for.

Perhaps the pastor understood what he meant, but there was no further time to discuss it, for he had to excuse himself to meet with the board concerning new cribs for the nursery.

How many missionaries have discovered this type of response, even in their own home churches? Oh, the checks arrived every month. You see, it isn't too difficult to write a check once every four weeks. But that is the extent of their involvement.

Ask any missionary you meet, "What is your greatest need?" Almost to a man they will reply, "We need prayer partners." Some mission boards have a rule that no missionary can leave for the field until he has a minimum of 100 or 500 prayer supporters. Finances are necessary. Equipment is important. Travel expenses must be met. But without adequate prayer backing, a missionary will be a failure.

Perhaps you are not a full-time prayer warrior. We need those who are committed to the ministry of prayer in this capacity. But all of us can give some prayer support, not to everyone we meet, but to those special ones whom God lays upon our hearts. It is far better to pray faithfully for one or two than to pray spasmodically that God will bless His work and His workers worldwide.

Now, if you are to pray specifically for a certain few, how should you go about it? To pray effectively, be ready to become acquainted with those for whom you pray. This may come through personal contact or correspondence. Show a sincere interest in your missionary. Ask him what his prayer requests are. Keep informed and up to date on his needs.

Apart from those requests peculiar to each missionary for whom you pray, remember to uphold him in an overall, general way as well.

Many a missionary career has come to an untimely halt because of health problems. Disease, stress, breakdowns are the rewards of some workers. Many serve not only in a spiritually hostile area, but certainly in a physically debilitating one. With sickness and disease surrounding them, some missionaries must be constantly on guard against that glass of insufficiently boiled milk; the polluted cup of water; the hazards of undercooked vegetables, of overkept meat, of all that insufficient refrigeration and sanitation will produce. Mingling with the crowds, eating in village homes, treating others who are unwell and have contagious diseases—all this increases the possibility of physical ailments. Pray for the health of your missionary. Pray, too, that he will not become too careless in this area, disregarding all safety precautions.

Emotions can be problems among missionary personnel. Remember, they are ordinary human beings! Some become so involved in their ministry that their family is neglected. The intensity of the work and the involvement with people and their problems cause a constant emotional drain. Tempers can flare. Getting along with others can be a problem. There is much joy in missionary service, but there are also hard times and difficult situations.

How would *you* feel if you were asked to leave the country? How would *you* react if word came that there was a reward out to anyone who would take your life? What would *you* do if you stood amid rock-throwing, blaspheming mobs as you preached Christ? What would *your* reaction be if you had worked for ten years among Muslim people and had a total of three converts—and two of those turned back? How would you feel if *you* had to leave your thirteen-year-old son in the States for education because there was no school anywhere in your area? What would it do to *you* if a cable should arrive stating simply, "Mother called Home," and you are 10,000 miles distant? What if *you* should happen upon a group of chanting individuals, writhing in a frenzied dance, cutting themselves with chains and knives until they are reeling and bleeding and fainting? Yes, missionaries do face situations of this kind. Pray for your missionary's emotional health.

Decision making is the constant course of the life of your missionary. He must have suitable answers to satisfy his own needs. He must be able to counsel those who come to him for help. How does a new convert with four wives begin life in Christ? Where should the new station be built? Should the money in the work account be used for a ceiling in the fourth-grade classroom or to make screens for the missionary bungalow? Should you teach several small or large groups of people, or should you concentrate on one group and train them to teach others? Should you take time to do literacy work? The missionary may receive help from his field director in some of these matters. Or perhaps he *is* the field director. Often he is far away from help of this kind. Spur-of-the-moment decisions have to be made. (Should I operate on the patient, or send him to the city where there are better facilities? It takes eight hours to get there over gravel roads, and he could die on the way. Yet this is not my field of surgery.) Yes, your missionary needs your prayers that he will make the best decisions in every problem or question which arises.

Do you ever wake up in the morning, find it pouring rain, dismal, humid, unpleasant? "What a nice day to curl up with a book and spend the day in bed," you say. It does not always take miserable weather to produce depression, but it helps! Your missionary may be in an area where monsoon rains arrive periodically. The sun is hidden from view for six to eight weeks. The washed clothes never get dry. Books begin to mold. The children have to stay indoors. Important outside activities must be put off.

Or perhaps the problem is heat. Imagine yourself anchored in the desert where 120° temperatures are the norm nine months of the year, where even the slightest sprinkle of rain brings great joy and the whole family runs outside to enjoy it; and water is scarce. The garden dries up and withers away.

Or perhaps the cold is pressing in. The mountains of Alaska are covered with foot upon foot of snow. Even the mail plane is unable to get through for several weeks.

Or what about your missionary living with that small tribe out in the jungle—with no means of transportation, no stores, no one of his own race within 500 or 1,000 miles. He teaches his own children the Calvert course or some other correspondence school material. He has to go out to the city twice a year (500 miles each way). The joy of at last getting mail is subdued by that fact that he must return to his station as soon as possible before his home is looted, burned, or destroyed by driver ants.

All the discontentments, discouragements, distresses, and disappointments of thwarted hopes along with the despondence and depression of aloneness, weariness, and problems which seem to have no answers press in upon your missionary. Pray for your missionary's psychological health.

Items for prayer never are lacking: the need for funds, both for monthly support and special projects; the missionary children attending schools away from their parents; those who teach them, and the "aunties" and "uncles" who mother and father them during their absence from home; that no harm may come in the way of accident or injury; that tensions in the home may be readily solved; that dealing with servants may not be an unpleasant experience; that no robberies cause the removal or destruction of valuable tools or equipment; that an adequate language teacher may be found to give help in language study; that the language might be learned quickly, well, and idiomatically; that jealousies might not develop within the group; that the rapport and spirit between missionaries and nationals might be mutually agreeable and beneficial. Pray for your missionary as you would pray for yourself and your family. Make him a part of your fellowship in both personal and family devotions.

Above all, your missionary is striving against the power of Satan in a way you may never experience or recognize. His battles with the powers of darkness are very real. Not only is he in the enemy's territory, he may be away from Christian friends, Christian literature, Christian fellowship, and every source of spiritual strength he once relied upon. He may have become spiritually dry or unfruitful. Bible reading may have had to take second or third place in his priorities. Prayer may have been neglected. God may seem remote and untouchable. The heavens may seem as brass. If you remember to pray for nothing else, pray for the spiritual health of your missionary.

Do you remember to pray, too, for the fruit of the witness your missionary gives? For his national co-workers? How seldom we pray earnestly for our brothers and sisters in Christ who sometimes put their very lives in jeopardy by accepting Jesus as their Saviour. They need your prayer fellowship in a very real way as they face dangers and persecution you may never be called upon to endure. Many are completely dependent upon the Holy Spirit to teach them. Some cannot read nor write. The missionary may move on to a new area and leave converts who have been taught very little beyond the basics of salvation. They desperately need your prayerful concern.

Many missionaries are working with people who have no background in or knowledge of Christianity. This means that the missionary must teach and live fundamental beliefs. He must be absolutely sure of his own doctrinal position. He must be ready always to give an answer to those who inquire.

He must have a knowledge of the language of the people among whom he works, or he will become frustrated and ineffective.

The ministry of prayer is as vital as a transfusion to one who has lost a lot of blood. Without your support in this way, the work of your missionary will suffer.

It has been stated that these days, they just don't make many missionaries like William Carey. Carey changed the whole history of India and missions two hundred years ago. Yet few people have ever heard of Carey's sister, paralyzed and bedridden for fifty years. Although unable to speak for much of that period, with great effort, she allowed herself to be propped up in bed. She wrote long, encouraging letters to her brother. And she prayed for him several hours each day—for *fifty years!*

It may be true that the William Careys are few and far between today. But have you thought that the reason for this could be that there are too few sisters praying and encouraging their missionary brothers?

The next time a missionary stands in your midst and pleads, "Pray for us," be assured these are not idle words. They are fraught with meaning. They are intended as an invitation. They are expressed in the hope that one or more in the congregation will take up the challenge.

In God's economy, the one who prays is as important as the one who goes. The one who stays shares in all of the joys, sorrows, victories, and defeats of the servant who sets sail for missionary service. As David said by the inspiration of God, "As his part is that goeth down to the battle, so shall his part be that tarrieth by the stuff: they shall part alike." (1 Sa 30: 24). *You* have a responsibility to your missionary in the matter of prayer. Therefore, "Continue in prayer, and watch in the same with thanksgiving" (i.e., don't forget to give praise, Col 4:2). "Pray without ceasing" (1 Th 5:17). Be encouraged in your ministry, for the promise is, "And all things, whatsoever ye shall ask in prayer, believing, ye shall receive" (Mt 21:22) . What an encouragement you can be to your missionary when you enter into prayer partnership with him. Your missionary needs your help. Pray not only that God will answer his prayers, but that he will make and take time to pray; not only that he will be kept from sickness and temptation, but that God will be glorified and triumphant even in these; not that he may have a rose-strewn pathway, but that he may experience God's sufficiency in spite of difficulties; not only that the mountains of fear and other obstacles be removed, but that he might find God's strength to climb above and overcome them; not only that God will bless his work, but that he might ever be faithful in the tasks committed to him. Pray for your missionary, remembering he is tempted with the same passions, pride, and prejudices that you are. Pray not only for great results of his endeavors, but that he may be zealous to serve and have a deep, insatiable passion to introduce the lost to Jesus Christ.

> Do you know what happened on that day,
> When burdened for souls you tried to pray?
> Did you think you'd failed to reach God's throne
> When your lips were dumb, your prayer a groan?
>
> Over the sea in a hot, dry land,
> A sower sowed with a faltering hand.
> But lo, in that hour refreshing came.
> God's servant found new strength again.
>
> And souls long held in the grip of sin
> Turned from despair to new life in Him.
> Away from their bondage they turned to God,
> And found their peace through Jesus' blood.
>
> For your faith had touched God's mighty hand—
> And the rains came down in a desert land.
>
> AUTHOR UNKNOWN

2

FINANCIAL PARTNERSHIP

Dollars can go to work for missions in a multitude of ways. Some churches give to a unified budget; some give specified sums annually to their denominational missionary projects; some individuals choose to give funds to organizations and individuals on a one-time basis or as the appeal strikes their emotional situation at the moment; others support specific missionaries or mission boards; some choose to support a different missionary each year from among those who have been pledged support through the church. Many Christians have never felt they should give a cent toward overseas work "because there is so much yet to be done at home." Others put a token offering in the missions portion of their church envelope as a matter of habit or conscience.

Fortunately, some people take the matter of missionary giving very seriously. They not only resolve to put their finances to work in the service of the Lord, but they want to know where their money is going and what it is accomplishing. This makes excellent business sense, and certainly should be expected in the Christian world. Accountability is imperative! A report concerning expenditures of mission funds should be available to each church member and contributor, whether it be a denominational project or personalized support.

Whether you give little or much, it is a fairly simple task to write a check or put a bill in the offering plate. Few of us have ever given a truly sacrificial offering, one which caused us to go without a necessity in order to meet another's need. For many, a missionary contribution is not only a token gift, but it is given with the same attitude as one who receives a wedding invitation from a mere acquaintance. A sense of obligation causes him to send a gift, even though he may not attend the ceremony.

As Christians, we have been taught to give our gifts and offerings to the Lord. But one of the most difficult areas of our lives to commit to Him is our money. We seem to have the impression that this, indeed, is *ours*. We are willing to give to those whom we know—our loved ones and friends—but to give simply for a cause with no promise of gratitude, love, and reciprocation does not appeal to us so much. We are more willing to become financially involved in something to perpetuate our name or our memory. We all like an occasional pat on the back, and an acknowledgment that our contribution has been of benefit, or that we have met a need. To give to an unknown person or a cause in which we have minimal interest lacks gratification. Thus, many people give because it is the thing to do or because it lessens the income tax.

Although I must mention these rather negative aspects of financial giving, I want to stress the fact that hundreds of thousands of Christians have discovered a true and meaningful ministry by using their funds for the Lord's work. They give as unto Him, they entrust it to Him and His work. And because of such faithful stewardship, the gospel of Jesus Christ has been preached around the globe.

Now, how *can* you receive personal satisfaction from giving to missions? One of the best ways is to give support to missionaries you know, or to those whom you are willing to get to know. This is easily done when your church operates a faith-promise plan of missionary support, or you give directly to a mission board for the support of a missionary or a project you select, or you give through your church, designating your gifts to a specific purpose. This is probably not possible in a situation where you give to a unified missions budget which, in turn, is given to a higher board of missions within the denomination, by which funds are designated at their discretion. Nevertheless, it is possible to become more personally involved in your giving by asking that board to supply you with the name of an individual or group for which your funds are used. Then you will feel part of all that has been accomplished in this way.

If you believe in missions, if you are to obey our Lord's last command, if you are to participate in a satisfying ministry, become involved in a financial partnership with those who are carrying out the Great Commission. Become personally acquainted with those to whom you give. Ask for reports of what your dollars are accomplishing, but don't expect the missionary to account for every dime. Prayerfully seek God's will concerning what area of work He wants you to become involved in. Don't support orphans *just* because you feel sorry for them. Don't support a cause *just* because your pastor thinks you should. Don't support a new project *just* because it sounds exciting. Support something you can give to wholeheartedly, cheerfully, as unto the Lord. Follow your gifts with your prayers and interest. Don't let your support become a mere habit, another bill to be paid, another obligation to be met. Give willingly and generously.

If you should choose to support an individual missionary, you will find that your relationship with this person can become one of the most satisfying experiences of your entire life. One sows, another waters, and God gives the increase. But each step is important and vital.

But some readers will say, "I have so little to give." Do you remember the quotation, "Little is much when God is in it"? God does not require a large portion from us if we do not have much to give. He never demands more than He can fulfill through us. Therefore, be grateful for the little you are able to contribute. Ask the Lord to multiply it. Perhaps you can contribute only a dollar or two a month to missions. Don't withhold a widow's mite simply because you are embarrassed to give so little, or because you feel it is not enough to bother with. A lady I once knew put ten cents in the offering plate each Sunday morning. She once said to me, "I know it's only a little, but if *everyone* gave that much, there's no end to what could be done." I thought about that and tried to figure how much our little church would receive in a week if everyone put a dime in the plate at the two Sunday services, or Sunday school and morning worship. It would not amount to nearly what we were presently receiving, but all would have some participation. Suppose each person in your congregation were to give his normal tithe and offerings to the church and then add just another ten cents each week designated for missions. And suppose 500 people attended your services. You could actually support a missionary for a year with these funds.

A few of you may be able to take on the full support of a missionary. Others will be able to give a portion of his support. Many will be able to give smaller gifts designated for an individual. No matter how much or how little you contribute, he will be *your* missionary—a living, personal reality. You will have entered into financial partnership with him.

Perhaps some of my readers have not yet entered into the joy of giving to a missionary. This person may be serving Him at home or overseas. God gives no greater rewards to those who support a missionary in the jungles of Brazil than those who support a mission administrator in the homeland. Both are necessary.

Financial partnership is only one of a thousand ways in which you are able to participate in the missionary outreach of the church. But if you have missed out on the blessing of this program, why not step out in faith and begin now? You can't afford to give? You can't afford *not* to give! It was Dr. Oswald J. Smith who said, "Let your giving be according to your means lest God make your means according to your giving."

Churches which have not taken a serious interest in the cause of missions are not completely fulfilling their purpose for existence. Upon His departure, the Lord said, "Ye shall be witnesses unto me both in Jerusalem, and in all Judea, and in Samaria, and unto the uttermost part of the earth" (Ac 1: 8). If you have lost your sense of mission, you are merely existing.

We need strong home bases, but these must be supply lines for those who are "lengthening the cords and strengthening the stakes" in the battle against the enemy of our souls. Behold, *now* is the accepted time; behold, *now* is the day of salvation. Let us, therefore, work while there is still time; for the night will soon be upon us, and it will then be eternally too late for many who could have been reached because of our financial partnership and faithful stewardship.

3

MORE ABOUT PERSONALIZED GIVING

When a person is confronted with the urgent needs of several organizations and individuals, he may have trouble deciding how he should invest his time, interest, and financial fellowship. Hardly a day passes that the mail does not bring requests for funds, perhaps from charities; perhaps from orphan children in underprivileged conditions at home and abroad; perhaps a personal letter comes with a mention of need for tuition money, business loan, or additional resources for the new baby's upkeep. It could be from a home or foreign mission board, a missionary, a Christian Bible school or college. It is often a plea for literature funds or money for a Christian radio station. On every hand, there are requests for financial assistance. Ninety-nine percent of the requests are for legitimate and worthy causes.

The usual response to financial needs comes only after all of an individual's personal needs have been met. This means that a very small amount is left for meeting obligations to others, even if a pledge or commitment has been made. Giving of that which is left over at the end of a month or a year will not go far in helping others. Perhaps you too have discovered this.

The only sure way to provide for giving is to budget a certain amount each month or from each paycheck. This works well if you are a strict budgeter. If you are lax in record-keeping, you will do best to pledge a set sum each week, month, or year which will become to you an obligation as certain as any bill you receive for services rendered.

Perhaps some readers are now thinking that this type of giving is no longer a free-will offering! Indeed it is not, *if* you give simply out of a sense of duty—or as a means of reducing income tax payments. But I am speaking to those of you who have a mind and willingness to give but never seem to have the necessary cash to carry through on your desire. Determine how much you can and want to use for the work of the Lord. According to God's request in the Old Testament Scriptures, He felt people should support His work to the extent of 10% of all they received. Since the tithe included jewelry, cattle, crops, and money, it would seem plausible that today this would include not only an individual's salary, but also payment received from interest, dividends, redemption of stocks and bonds, income tax refunds, inheritances, and special gifts received. If each of us were to give to the Lord this basic 10% of all we receive during a year, there would be little need for His workers to plead for additional funds to carry on their ministries.

There are some things in the Christian life that are not easily explained. How we know that God exists is one question with no easy answer. God is. By faith we accept it. But to prove it is impossible. I would like to include the area of giving in such a category. There is an unwritten rule that works out in life. The more you give, the more you have; the less you give, the less you have. In some mysterious way, God adds by dividing. It is impossible to write out the formula with pen and ink. Attempts at explaining how it works would be unsuccessful. But I submit to you that if you want to have more than you have ever had before, start giving to the work of the Lord, at least a tithe. Gifts and offerings above this basic amount then follow as you see God provide not only *your* needs but abundantly supply for others also. In this, we are reminded of what happened to those who were given talents to be kept or invested. Those who used theirs gained a hundredfold, but the one who hid his, lost even what he had.

I submit this to you for your serious consideration. I ask you to try it for yourself. Step out by faith and begin to give willingly and freely and cheerfully to God (for the Lord loves a cheerful giver, 2 Co 9:7). By personal commitment, prove it. You will discover that when you cast your bread upon the waters, it will come back to you cake—with icing!

Having determined how much you can give or pledge to the work of the Lord, it is then necessary to invest in those persons or projects which will produce satisfaction and eternal dividends to your account (not forgetting your contribution to your local church for its ministry and outreach). Whether you give to a united church missions fund or to individual enterprises, enter wholeheartedly into it. Ask questions. Make sure you know who or what you are supporting. And as you prove the truth of what you have just read, testify to others concerning it. Your enthusiastic involvement is the best advertising for others to join a going, growing program.

At a missionary conference, I heard this statement, which applies to every area of Christian living, including the stewardship of our money: "When we are what God wants us to be, we will do what God wants us to do."

4

LETTER WRITING

"As cold waters to a thirsty soul, so is good news from a far country" (Pr 25:25).

In this country, the mailman visits our box six days a week. True, he often leaves us bills, but he also brings us letters from friends and loved ones. Some people watch from one mail delivery to the next in anticipation of an expected communication, whether it be the monthly Social Security check, the program of coming events at symphony hall, or a promised note from a friend.

If the mailman does not produce the long-awaited letter, we are apt to get on the phone and dial a distant number as easily as a local one.

We are so accustomed to having around us radios, televisions, news magazines, friends, and church contacts, that we take for granted the availability of all these sources of news and fellowship. It becomes a question of what to hear or watch, or where to go next, or whom to talk to, when so many choices face us.

Your missionary, wherever he may be assigned to service, may be back in the pony express era. He is separated, even by telephone, from home and loved ones, the things that are most dear to him, neighbors, friends, church, town, and country. Many do not even have the advantage of a radio, or if they do, there is little time to tune in on English broadcasts. Magazines from home are scarce. Home, in fact, seems miles and years away.

34

Some missionaries are fortunate enough to have excellent mail service. Most mail gets through; some may be censored. In West Pakistan, for example, in the mid-1950s, it was my experience to have the *dak walla* (mailman) deliver mail twice a day, seven days a week. But I have had friends who worked in the jungles of South America who received mail only two or three times in a whole year.

Think how lonely you would become if you had no contact with home folks for five to eight months! This, of course, is not the norm, but some missionaries do have this problem. Others have fast, excellent deliveries. Tokyo, for example, has a rapid mail system, and letters reach destinations throughout the city in short order.

Whether the mail is delivered twice a day or twice a year, it will have no meaning to your missionary if no letters have been written!

Perhaps you do not know your missionary very well. Your first response will be, "But what can I write to him?" What do you write to your friends? You write about the weather, your new job, the baby's first words and steps, Grandma's ninetieth birthday party, the new neighbors, the church, who's engaged to whom, how you feel about women's lib, and so on. Then consider your missionary a friend. Tell him about the little things as well as the big events. Give him some national news. If something happens of great import, send along the newspaper clippings. Enclose a church bulletin or the program from Jon's recital. Send along some cartoons or jokes. A friend once wrote me from her place of service as houseparent in the school for missionary children. "Help!" she wrote. "If I'm to exist here, I've got to have some jokes and riddles for these kids." I was superintendent of the junior high department of our Sunday school, and the following week, I gave the group an assignment: Write down your favorite jokes and riddles so we can send them to a missionary. The following Sunday, I had over fifty items to send to my friend. Just a little thing, but I wish you could have read the letter of thanks we received in sincere gratitude.

While you are writing, ask questions. Find out the names and ages of the missionary's children. Find out if there is anything they would like to have, and if there is anything you can do for them.

From my own missionary experience, I can verify the fact that news from home—no matter who sends it—is a welcome sight. It is now a good many years since I went overseas, but I still correspond regularly with several families from various areas, folks I met briefly at the close of a meeting, some whom I have never met personally, but who are still my correspondents today.

Send pictures of yourself and your family. Let your children write notes to their children. Be cheerful and optimistic. It is good to share news, but it can be disheartening to receive only bad tidings. Do find *some*thing that will be good news to the receiver!

The wide use of tape recorders affords an opportunity to send news which is even more personal than a written letter. The tape can include news from the entire family, the anthem your choir sang, or a favorite song.

I remember when a friend of co-workers on our field once received an envelope marked "Taped Letter." We were all invited to hear the "letter," so we gathered in the large living room of our mud bungalow, and the tape was turned on. To our surprise, no one spoke. But for twenty minutes, this friend had recorded laughter, first just one individual, then a group, and finally an entire congregation. No sooner had the tape started than one, then another, and then the entire room was laughing. We laughed until we hurt, and the tape had to be turned off! It was a silly thing, I suppose, but you can't imagine how much it relieved our tensions and brought us together. After that, when the going got rough, we had only to remember the tape, and we would smile.

Solomon said, "A merry heart doeth good like a medicine: but a broken spirit drieth the bones" (Pr 17:22). This does not mean that your communications should contain nothing but trivia. But a good dose of optimism will produce joy in the heart of a missionary far from loved ones.

Missionaries serving at home need to hear from you, too. Encourage them. Make them know you are remembering them and supporting them by your interest and prayers.

You may not have the money to provide several dollars toward the support of your missionary. This should not keep you from staying in touch. For those of you who do give money, this does not end your duty. It is absolutely essential that you write, too.

There will be times when your missionary does not write to you. (Some missionaries, like many other people, just aren't writers.) Duties may prohibit him; time may not allow it. Keep these factors in mind. Don't wait for a reply from your missionary before writing again. Unknown to you, your letters have lightened a load and brought joy to a heart, even though you may not have heard about it.

If you ask a missionary what he wants most, his answer will be "Prayer." If you should ask him what comes next on his list, he would probably say "Mail." Don't disappoint him, on the field or during his furlough.

Long, articulate, personal letters have become a thing of the past in our busy, long-distance world. But if writing letters has become a lost art, it can be revived. It may be difficult to get those first few words to run out of your trusty ballpoint, but the advice given to would-be professional writers is excellent: *Write!* The longer you put it off, the less you will feel like doing it. Write as though you were having a face-to-face encounter with your missionary friend. If you were speaking to him, you would think of a number of questions beginning with, "Did you know—" and "Have you heard—" Just put them down on paper.

Ever find yourself making excuses? "No one can read my writing." Try typing. "I don't know how much postage the letter will take." Ask at the post office. "I don't know what to say." If someone was starving, would you stand there debating what to feed him? Your missionary may be mail starved.

After you have written your letter, be sure to send it off as soon as possible, and send it via air mail. Regular mail can take several months to reach its destination. Perhaps you have heard of missionaries who are still receiving Christmas cards in March. Well, bless the hearts of those who cared enough to send a greeting. But next year, try air mail. It costs so little extra and assures you that it will be received on time.

As much as letters are appreciated, missionaries also enjoy receiving greetings for birthdays, anniversaries, and other special occasions. Remember that Thanksgiving, Labor Day, Independence Day, Washington's birthday, and some of our other legal holidays are typically American. Although your missionary may be eating his usual slice of water buffalo meat on Thanksgiving Day, your card will remind him that back home, families are gathering together, football is at its zenith, and turkeys are roasting all over the country. Even Christmas may not be what he had expected. If he is in a non-Christian land, there will be no reminders of Christ's birth. It will just be another date on the calendar: no carols, no trees, no gifts, no cards, no tinsel, no tableaux, no snow, no jingle of bells, no Salvation Army appeals. A missionary can still celebrate Christ's birth without these familiar external things, but Christmas greetings do bring cheer, nevertheless.

Missionaries appreciate some of the better, humorous, contemporary cards. They appreciate it when someone sends them something other than "God bless you in His service" cards. They also appreciate picture postcards, and surely you can write *that* much!

Do not wait for the pastor to write, nor old Mrs. King who

really cannot have any other ministry, nor Sally Jo who is confined to bed with a broken hip, nor Jim who is used to writing letters since he has to do so many at work, or anyone else who seems a likelier letter-writer. They may never do it! So *you* lead the way. How I wish it were possible for you to be on the other end when the letter arrives and your missionary says to his family, "Guess who we heard from!"

Do your missionary a favor. Write him a letter *today.* Make sure you write correctly all the numbers and letters in his address. (I once received a letter addressed to me at West Pakistan, India, South America!) And be sure to enclose your return address. You may be pleasantly surprised some day to find an answer to your letter sitting in your mailbox.

Sometimes they smile at her and ask her why
She tries to make a prompt, complete reply
To every letter she receives, no matter
How full of odd requests and aimless chatter
They are, or how it hinders getting through
With all the other things she has to do.

She smiles at them, but does not often speak
Of having learned how lonely people seek
For friends by mail, and count the hours till some
Reply, however trivial, might come—
Or how a heart may, all its days, go lame
Because a certain letter never came.

JANE MERCHANT

5

VISIT YOUR MISSIONARY

Once you have established a relationship with your missionary, you will be anxious for him to visit you during his furlough. You will anticipate the reunion and fellowship and letting him get to know you and your family better.

Have you ever thought of this procedure being reversed? We live in an age when travel is common. A trip to the Continent seems as near as next door. Friends may be busy planning a flight to South America, a cruise to the islands, or a world trip. Many folks get away without leaving this country by visiting our national parks, oceanside resorts, or Indian reservations. We are a mobile people, and most jobs allow at least a two-week vacation period per year, with more time available if requested in advance. The expense of travel has been greatly reduced in many cases, so that trips abroad are sometimes no more expensive than visiting another state. Perhaps you have already enjoyed international touring in the past and are looking forward to seeing other places in the future. Or it could be that you have never ventured far from home, but would like to plan such a trip.

Why not consider your missionary in your plans? Missionaries work in some of the most beautiful spots in the world. Many are off the beaten track of tourist trails, which makes them even more pleasant to visit. Your missionary will give you a royal welcome. Visitors from home are always treated to the best of everything: those tins of Spam being saved for a special feast, a tour of out-of-the-way villages, the loving warmth and fellowship of fellow missionaries (if there are any in the area), and that firsthand meeting with the people of the land in which your missionary serves. Worshiping with brothers and sisters in Christ, under their leadership, in their places of worship (whether sitting under a tree in the desert sand or in the pew of a straw building, or in a mud and mortar cathedral), even though the language may not be understood, will bring a heart kinship to these friends in Christ.

It is good to see your missionary in his working situation; view his field and see people rather than a project, a ministry rather than a mission, intelligent people rather than illiterate nonentities; meet nationals who are not just poor pagans, but rich and middle-class people, perhaps Christian, perhaps steeped in their own religion. You can expect to meet not just Indians out in the jungles or naked savages in the bush, but fully clothed, often Western-influenced individuals in some of the most beautiful cities of the world. Missions are not just for the underprivileged people, living in remote parts of the world. Missions are also reaching the overprivileged and common people wherever they may be found. You never thought of Paris, London, Rome, and Lucerne as places of missionary endeavor? What about Tokyo, Hong Kong, Singapore, and New Delhi? Or Rio, Quito, Mexico City, or Quebec? And don't forget Boston, New York, Miami, and San Francisco. Not all missionaries are serving in faraway places. Not all of God's servants are even ministering overseas.

Perhaps your budget will not allow you to go far from home. You may still be able to visit the work among the Seminoles in Florida, Navajo work in Arizona, or Jewish evangelism ministries in one of many areas of the country. If your missionary serves in a remote place of the world, visit another missionary nearer home. You will still be able to picture better his joys and needs.

With a little planning and advice, you may be able to visit folks farther away. Many mission societies today provide you with an opportunity to visit the foreign field. You go on a chartered flight with a well-known airline. You have the fellowship of a large group of Christians with whom you travel. You have the benefit of a guide who takes care of a zillion and one details of your trip so that you have no responsibilities other than to be at an appointed place at the designated hour. You see more of the field and the work than you could on your own. You may have the advantage of seeing more than one area of the work. You are able, in most cases, to live with missionary families and get a feel of their work. You are introduced to nationals whom you will come to know, love, appreciate, and pray for. You will be sure to have the most sanitary living conditions available, and your food and water will be carefully prepared in order to avoid the physical maladies which can come from careless preparation and serving.

Yet, even a well-planned tour will not give you a full insight into the work and life of your missionary. It is, however, an excellent plan, and certainly saves time, energy, red tape, complications, and money.

On the other hand, if you enjoy looking at maps, routing yourself from place to place, visiting areas you have never even heard of, plan your own missionary itinerary. It can be a very enjoyable process. Write to your missionary and ask when it would be best for you to visit. (He may be aware of conditions which you might not consider, such as, summer monsoons, winter blizzards, hot spells.) Then decide on your routing. If you have several friends serving in many areas, include as many stops as possible on your tour but allow sufficient time with each to say more than hello between planes. Try to stay a week in each country you visit, even though you may be in several places within the nation during that time.

If you travel by air, you are usually allowed stopovers at several points at little or no extra charge. For example, if you are flying across northern India and have no missionary contacts in Agra, do not let this be a cause for your missing the Taj Mahal!

After making tentative plans for your trip, let a reputable travel agency do the actual paper work for you. They can give invaluable aid in getting tickets, accommodations, visas, and entrance papers for you. They will tell you what procedures to follow in getting your health card validated. They will get you the most direct routes, the least expensive modes of travel, and they usually do it in near record time. They are aware of discount fares, off-season rates, and family plans. They can arrange for any kind of itinerary and will see that each step is confirmed, including hotel accommodations where you may not have missionary friends. Although I would not advise it for everyone, four of us were able to arrange a six-week, around-the-world jaunt, within five weeks of our departure date, including visits to Hawaii, Tokyo, Hong Kong, Thailand, India, West Pakistan, Aden, Ethiopia, Egypt, and England. Amazing though it may seem, there was not one delay in our travel; all accommodations were prepared for us, and we enjoyed twenty-three separate flights in foreign lands, with no problem with customs or flights overseas. (In our own country we had a delay on the West Coast as our plane was searched because of a bomb threat, and six weeks later on the East Coast, our plane depressurized at 36,000 feet, initiating an emergency landing. We began to think our missionaries lived in the safer places!)

A visit with your missionary will bring about an awareness of his surroundings, his ministry, his family, and his personal goals and needs. You will begin to understand why he has never mentioned some of his routine problems in public meetings. You will see what a busy schedule he keeps and how he is called upon at any time for work, advice, or counsel. You will hear him speak in his new language; you will share food which, although it sounded unpalatable when mentioned in furlough meetings, is really very tasty and filling. (Most folks easily digest fish eyes, octopus, and monkey meat!) You may drink creamy, rich, water-buffalo milk. You will eat home-baked bread. You will probably enjoy morning coffee and afternoon tea. That early afternoon siesta may be quite a joy, too.

I have known some folks who have visited their missionary and come away with the feeling that he is better off than he should be! (Somehow we have the feeling that missionaries live on a shoestring support system, and therefore they must not have anything too nice!)

Others have come away with the impression that missionaries spend all their time eating and entertaining. This may be particularly so in the case of those who join a tour group. Little do the tour members know about how the missionaries have canned fruits and vegetables and hidden away goodies which arrived in packages from home so they could treat their guests to familiar "home style" food. No missionary wants to kill his guests during the first meal with burning hot curry; few even want to offer bear or camel meat until the home folks are more fully acclimatized.

Then there are those who feel that a missionary really has it made with all the servants he has at his disposal. (Why is it that servants are always on good behavior when friends from home arrive?) Little does the visitor know how difficult life would be without household help. In fact, no other work could be accomplished. The casual viewer can hardly understand the time and patience which goes into each servant's training, and the problem of loyalty; as soon as they are trained, some servants will leave for a higher paying position with someone else. No one will ever know how much has been lost permanently because of unreliable servants. Neither can one imagine the harm done by reprimanded servants who have retaliated by spreading untrue stories about the missionaries. (Perhaps some missionaries do not know how to

manage servants and thus they bring on a great deal of grief.)
Yet the need for servants remains, so do not envy the missionary that privilege. You, too, would need such help in their
circumstances. In fairness, let me add that many faithful
servants would be willing to give their very lives for the missionary whom they serve.

Most people who come back from a visit to the mission
field are changed individuals. Never before had there been
a realization of the field as it actually exists. Prayer support
is activated and becomes far more personal and specific. These
visitors have seen some of the material needs of their missionary. Perhaps they were delighted to be able to supply that
need, or they were able to come home to friends and church
and stir them to contribute to a fund for a new generator, a
light plant, a vehicle in good repair, or a refrigerator.

Unless you truly desire to become involved more deeply
and personally in missionaries and their work, *don't* visit
them in their places of service. But if you long for more
depth in your prayer support and financial backing, plan
your visit and follow through on your plans as soon as
you can.

One of the finest gifts, by the way, that your church can
give its pastor and his wife is a trip to visit one (or several)
of your church missionaries at their place of service. In most
cases, your pastor and your church will benefit a thousandfold
as a result, and this, in turn, will help your missionary.

Just one warning must be mentioned. The world in which
your missionary lives and moves and has his being does not
stop because you happened to have arrived on his doorstep.
You may want him to give you a guided tour through his
area; introduce you to everyone, and explain everything. His
necessary work may prohibit him from spending every hour of
every day with you. The more warning you give him of your
arrival, the more likely it will be that he can plan his schedule

with your visit in mind. He will do his utmost to accommodate you. But his classes, outpatient clinic, operating room schedule, literacy program, broadcasts, secretarial work, or administrating must go on in spite of your presence. Keep this in mind as you plan your visit.

6

SOME ABCs FOR HELPING MISSIONARIES ON THE FIELD

In many lands, no amount of money could purchase some of the everyday items we consider necessities, such as Scotch tape, clothespins, detergents, or paper napkins. And serving in those areas are more than 35,000 American missionaries. In this chapter, I want to share with you just a skeleton outline of some of those things which you can provide for missionaries, thus lightening their load and lifting their spirits.

Before I list these ABCs, however, certain statements and guidelines should be set down. These will not only help you as you minister to your missionary acquaintances and friends, but they will eliminate some of the problems that arise when interested supporters unwittingly hinder rather than help missionaries by overlooking some important factors related to sending gifts overseas.

The most common item sent to missionaries is money. Although it would seem likely that gifts of money would be of much help to those serving overseas, such funds must never be sent directly to the missionary in cash. It is not only illegal in at least two ways (it is against US government regulations, and in many countries, all foreign currency must be reported as the missionary enters the country; otherwise it is illegal currency) ; but there is only a slim possibility that cash dollars will safely reach their destination. Personal checks sometimes go through the mails safely, but in some countries, mail is

47

censored, and any enclosures in letters are confiscated. Unfortunately, there are black-market banks in some areas where stolen checks can be cashed by any bearer upon demand. Then too, many times, a missionary is unable to cash a foreign check unless he has an open bank account in the country where he serves. If he does not, he must chance returning the check to the homeland for servicing, thus multiplying the risk of its being lost.

The only safe way to transmit your funds for use by your missionary is to send a check to the home office of his mission board. If it is for his necessary support, be sure to specify this fact and clearly indicate the name of the missionary to whom it should be assigned. If it is to provide equipment, transportation, or other need obligated by his work, designate it for his work account. In both of these cases, your gifts, at the present time, are fully tax deductible.

You may, on the other hand, simply want to send money as a love gift or personal gift to a missionary overseas. It may be for a birthday, anniversary, or Christmas; it may be for holiday expenses; it might be to purchase something on the field to brighten the life of the children in the family. These gifts too are best sent to the home office of the mission board under which your missionary serves. Be sure to designate them as "Personal Gift" and indicate to whom they should be sent. You can be sure that the board will transmit the entire gift to the designated recipient.

If your missionary assures you that the mail is reliable, you might ask if he would rather have you send a personal check directly to him rather than going through the home office. You will have to make the final decision concerning the transmission of funds in this case.

It is possible, of course, to send International Money Orders. This should also be checked with your missionary, however. In some countries, it will mean that upon receipt of the money order, the missionary will have to make a trip to the post office and go through an enormous amount of waiting and red tape in order to receive the funds.

Even though your money would considerably help the missionary, too often the money comes at a time when the national church has a special need, another orphan must be fed, a new convert is forced out of his job and needs help, and the purpose for which you sent the funds (i.e., the personal use of the missionary) never becomes a reality. It isn't that the missionary is guilty of misappropriation of funds, but perhaps a need has just arisen, and he had hoped to be able to share in providing the answer, but was unable to until your gift arrived. It seemed more necessary that the need of someone else should be met than that the missionary should use the money for his personal advancement.

Because of this, it is sometimes better to send things, other than dollars, to missionaries. But here, again, careful consideration must be given to this matter. Always check with your missionary before sending any item to him. Let him tell you if your choice of gift will be practical to him. (Developing countries in many parts of the world today are producing goods which may be as good or better than what you might send him.) Government restrictions on certain items may make it impractical for those things to be sent. Customs duty may be extremely high on all items entering the country, thus making the cost of receiving the parcel prohibitive for the missionary. Also, some countries allow no goods inside their borders unless they have previously issued a license for it. This means that unless a missionary has specifically requested an item and has the necessary license in hand, no goods will reach him. The items are confiscated and later sold at public auction or on the streets. So it is very important that you contact your missionary before sending him any type of parcel. Specify what you are planning to send. Then take his advice concerning if, how, and when to ship the items.

Some mission boards utilize the services of certain airlines

for charter flights, making it possible to transport large numbers of missionaries from one area of the world either to the
US, or to their country of service from the US. Some of these
flights are set up in such a way that extra baggage can be taken
at no additional cost. If you have items for a missionary, contact the board to see if it could be sent out with a returning
missionary in this manner. You can't do it with every board
and with every country, but it is certainly worth asking.

In some cases, first-time or returning missionaries are willing to take in packages for fellow missionaries. Do not pre-
sume upon anyone to do this for you. Be sure you have their
full permission. Make sure they know exactly what you would
like them to take for you. If the package is wrapped, be certain to mark on the outside the exact contents or send a list to
the one who has volunteered to deliver the package. (He
may have to declare the value and contents of the package
when he enters the country.)

Unless you have written to the mission board for permission, do not send gift parcels to them with a request that they
be sent on to the field. Although they are sympathetic to
both you and the missionary you want to supply, they are just
not set up to handle personal packages. Some boards do allow you to send small items (especially emergency items, e.g.,
eyeglass replacements, batteries for hearing aids or equipment, or sometimes even a wedding veil), and they will try
to send it along with the first missionary going to that country. If you do send packages to the board without their permission, they may return it to you COD. So be sure to check
with them on this matter.

If a missionary writes that the things you intend to send
will be of help to him, and he can receive gift packages in the
country where he serves, and if the postal service is reliable,
then go ahead and send the parcel. But before you purchase
the item, check with your local post office concerning any size
or weight regulations in effect for the country to which you

will be sending the items. Find out what tags must be attached to the box and what declarations must be made. You will always have to give a US dollar valuation of the things you send. Almost always, the lower your valuation, the less customs will be assessed. But you must assess a fair value on each item. Never declare the full *retail* value of an item. The wholesale value can legitimately be used. If you want to send clothing, run it through the washer. It is then used clothing with very little valuation. Some items (such as heavily used toys, dolls, or puzzles) should be itemized as NCV (no commercial value). Try to limit the total valuation on your package to less than ten dollars, US. You may also wish to mark clearly on the parcel: "Unsolicited Gift."

After purchasing the items for shipment, package them carefully. Dry foods (cake mixes, puddings, sugar, etc.) do well wrapped in aluminum foil or plastic bags. Avoid sending breakable jars unless they can be made "shock proof" with Styrofoam shavings. Never send mothballs and candy in the same package! Use plastic bags or aluminum foil as filler. It will protect your items and will be useful to the missionary (and does not have to be declared). Use a sturdy box, heavy wrapping paper, and strong string. Your package, even if marked "Fragile," will get more than one crash landing along the way!

The last step in the process is to take the package to the post office. Unless it is very light or very important, it will probably cost a small fortune to send it airmail. There are different classes and rates, however, so check on this possibility. The usual method of sending things is by parcel post. Make very sure your missionary's name with his correct and complete address is legibly written on the package. Your return address must also appear at the upper left-hand corner. The clerk will take it from there, and your package will be on its way.

Fortunately, there are still several free ports as well as several countries in the world where missionaries may receive most gifts with no problem with customs duty or government regulations. Find out if your missionary might just be in one of those areas.

Now that we have discussed the procedure for sending gifts abroad, perhaps we had better get on to that list of items which you may wish to consider purchasing, packaging, and parcel-posting to your missionary.

AUTOMOBILE

A jeep, Land Rover, or truck might be considered. Because a vehicle is an expensive item, requires (in most countries) special licenses and papers, and is dutiable, your missionary must be contacted for exact details concerning his need. If possible, send at least two extra tires; and as a special gift, send all or part of the expected duty expense to your missionary's board marked for that specific use by your missionary. (The major suppliers of motor vehicles can take care of exporting the vehicle at your request.) A vehicle makes a wonderful group gift. Missionary conferences sometimes provide sufficient funds to make it become a reality.

BABY THINGS

These are usually difficult to obtain on the field. If you know when the baby is due, it will help you plan to send your package so it will arrive at approximately the same time.

BIBLE

Many missionaries enjoy several versions of the Word of God for use in their devotional times. Some will welcome a new copy, for Bibles get hard use on the mission field. A reference Bible is extremely practical.

BICYCLE

In some areas of service, the use of a lightweight, two-wheeled vehicle is essential. Ask your missionary about this. Also, it may be better for him to purchase one on the field than for you to send him one from the States. If so, send the money, designated for him and for this specific item, to the home office of his mission board.

BOOKS AND MAGAZINES

Missionaries enjoy all kinds of reading material. Some will appreciate sermon outlines, others mystery stories, some devotional material, and others prefer light reading. Children too enjoy reading. The books do not have to be new. You probably have some on your shelves right now which could be sent. Overseas book-rate postage is one of the biggest dollar bargains of our times.

Most books will be passed along several times, or may end up in the mission headquarters or holiday home library for enjoyment by all.

As for magazines, besides Christian publications, missionaries enjoy those which give household hints, recipes, latest fashions, what's new in home decorating, news, and sports. These are also enjoyed and passed on to others. Don't forget the possibility of providing a subscription to your missionary's professional magazine. Both books and magazines can be sent overseas at amazingly low prices, and no duty is ever charged. Wrap a few books at a time in brown paper, tie them with string, and mark "Books" on the package. Roll magazines and send only two or three in a package.

CANDLES

A box of candles for use when the lights go out, for quiet dinners, or for birthday parties, is not available in many places. Wrap them in foil and pack them flat (unless your missionary has specified his preference for bent and misshapen wax!).

CHURCH BULLETINS

Your missionary is interested in what you and your church are doing for the Lord, just as you are interested in his ministry. Collect the bulletins and send them once a month.

CLOTHING

Perhaps you sew. Perhaps your ladies' group would like to make clothes for missionaries as a project. Ask first about color preferences. (Most folks will share information freely.) Get the proper sizes. Find out about special requirements. Sleeveless, low cut, and very short dresses are taboo for missionaries in most places. Or you may wish to provide material for the missionary to have made up into appropriate wearing apparel.

COAT HANGERS

We don't give them a moment's thought in the States, but try to purchase them in Bangkok! You probably have dozens you aren't using.

CORRESPONDENCE

This has been given a complete chapter in this book, but it is important enough to mention again. Keep in touch.

CURTAINS

These can often make a house a home; yet, they are often not available overseas.

DEVOTIONAL HELPS AND RESOURCE MATERIALS

Send articles, books, poems, or clippings which will provide help and inspiration. You don't have to preach in your letters, but devotional items can lighten a heavy heart. Also, ask your missionary if he needs any resource materials (such as flash cards, storybooks, slides, tapes, filmstrips, flannelgraph materials, etc.). He does not have resources at his disposal as you do. A visit to your public library might obtain an answer to one of his vital questions. Offer to help.

ENCYCLOPEDIA

Many parents purchase these when their children are young, but they are not used much after a while. A set could be invaluable to a missionary family, especially if they are in a remote area and the children must be taught by their parents.

FILM

You expect to see pictures your missionary has taken in his places of work, but often, he cannot obtain film easily where he is located. Find out what kind of a camera he has and what type of film he needs.

FIRST-AID BOOK

No home should be without one of these. Yet it is an item which many missionaries forget to take with them. Send a copy. They will be most grateful.

FUEL AND TRAVEL FUNDS

If your missionary has a vehicle of his own, it can be exceedingly expensive to keep it running. If he has to use public transportation, this too amounts to a considerable bit. Why not pledge money to his fuel and travel expenses just as you do to his personal support?

GAMES

We live life at such a pace that games are thought of as for children only. But on the mission field, games are both recreation and therapy for weary missionaries. Check with your missionary first, though. No matter how innocent the entertainment, in some situations, missionaries will not play games involving cards or dice.

GARDEN SEEDS

Be sure to check with your post office concerning regulations about sending seeds. If your missionary is allowed to receive them, a package of tomato or cucumber seeds, or zinnias and snapdragons may bring much joy to many when they come to fruition.

GREETING CARDS

All of us receive many cards in a year. The largest number probably accumulate at Christmastime. Your missionary may be able to use these greeting cards in many ways. Sometimes he will clip off the personal messages and reuse the cards. Often he will cut out the pictures and use them as prizes for children who say their memory verse or attend a meeting. These can be sent duty free at low cost. Be sure to mark the package, "Used greeting cards."

HOBBIES

Does your missionary, or do his children, have a stamp collection? Find out. If they do, be sure to use a variety of stamps on your letters. Then either enclose new issues as they come out, or purchase them and keep them at home to give him on his furlough. If *you* collect stamps, he will be glad to swap with you.

Women on the field love to try new dishes. But remember, they must utilize simple ingredients. Those that start with "Take one packaged mix," or "Take a pound of quick-frozen artichokes" will be useless. Send a new recipe each time you write. Clip these from newspapers or magazines, or take them from your personal file. Why not exchange recipes as a hobby?

Some lady missionaries are knitting fiends. If you were to sneak in on an annual mission meeting, your ears would be attuned to the clicking needles across the room. Find out if *your* missionary knits or crochets. Then supply her with needles, patterns, yarn, or thread.

LICENSES

If your missionary is a professional person whose license must be renewed periodically, handle it for him. Pay the fee, obtain the license, and send it to him, or have it sent from the agency. Drivers' licenses may also be kept validated in this way. (Check with your local registry of motor vehicles to see what can be done if a personal appearance is required for renewal. Many areas now require an eye and hearing or road test at certain intervals.)

MEDICINE

Prescriptions may be kept on file at home. You can volunteer to send them as needed. Special medicines also may be obtained. Check with your missionary, however. In some areas, medicines can be obtained right on the field at little expense with no difficulty. Some mission boards can supply medicines at very low cost to their missionaries. Although not strictly medicinal, items such as razor blades, toothpaste, toothbrushes, deodorant, and so on, may be appreciated.

MUSIC

Send music tapes—professional or parlor. Record some of your albums on tape. Record your choir at some of your church services. Classical and semiclassical music may be appreciated as much as strictly religious pieces. Your missionary may have a favorite song or musician. I remember a fellow from Ireland who would have given anything to hear some music from his homeland. It would be informative to the missionary to hear some of the sounds from the homeland that his ears will have to adjust to when he comes home on furlough!

NECESSARY EQUIPMENT AND TOOLS

Many missionaries could do a far more effective job if they had all the tools to work with. But they don't always make those needs known to the home folks. Ask every once in a while. You may be able to supply a very pressing need. A missionary learns to be a jack-of-all-trades. Don't be embarrassed to offer wrenches, screwdrivers, and a hammer to anyone.

PENS AND PENCILS

It's amazing how necessary these are. On a trip around the world to visit missionaries, we took one hundred ballpoint pens (advertising a bank and donated by one of its employees). Our supply was depleted on our first stop! Give your missionary a practical pen and pencil (and be sure to include refills).

PICTURES

Snapshots of you and your family, your community, or your church and its activities will be appreciated as your missionary comes to know you more personally. Pictures suitable for framing can also be sent to brighten up whitewashed walls.

PRAYER LETTERS

You can provide this service for your missionary. A later chapter will tell you how.

PUZZLES, JOKES, AND TOYS

Send puzzle books, jigsaw puzzles, and crossword puzzles or cryptograms (with answers) cut from the daily newspaper. Clip jokes and cartoons from magazines and newspapers. It is good therapy for your missionary. And don't forget the children. Toys are usually at a premium in missionary homes.

ROLLED BANDAGES

Although there seems to be less need and demand for bandages which have been made from torn sheets and shirts, it is possible that your missionary works in a situation where these would be of great use. Check on it.

SHOES

In many areas of the world, shoes which fit properly cannot be obtained at any price. I have a friend who wears a 14 EEEEE. Obviously, she cannot locate this size in Singapore!

SPORTS EQUIPMENT

Why not supply a badminton, croquet, or archery set? Tennis racquets and balls, a football, basketball, or baseball equipment might also be useful. Missionaries need recreation and enjoy it.

TAPES

We have already mentioned taped music. But what about a friendly taped letter, sermons, or just the home atmosphere with a bit of potpourri? Ask your missionary to return the favor.

TELEPHONE INSTALLATION

In some areas, a deposit of up to five hundred dollars is required for installation of a telephone. Perhaps you could provide the necessary amount, most of which would be returned when the line is disconnected. He could then use these funds for another needy situation.

WHITE ELEPHANTS

It may be junk to you, but you never know. Before discarding such items as lace doilies, old picture frames, or kitchenware, find out if they might be useful to a missionary.

WRITING AND WRAPPING PAPER

Want your missionary to write? Send a big hint. If the stationery is pretty, all the better! Then, too, your missionary will be the pride of his station and the center of attention when he receives a gift of wrapping paper for those special occasions on the field.

I have only scratched the surface as I've tried to set down some of the things that you can provide for your missionary on the field. It will take a bit of time and effort. It will mean writing to see what he needs, wants, and can receive. It will mean a call to the post office to get information. You will have to purchase the item (s), pack them, and get them on their way. None of this is impossible, though sometimes difficult. And surely, if you could stand at the side of your missionary when that parcel arrives, and see the joy on his face, you would be thrilled with the opportunity of providing him with some of those things that we too often take for granted here at home.

What your missionary needs will depend a great deal on where he is located, what type of work he is doing, what type of accommodations he has, what size and age his family is, whether he is married or single, and whether he is a home or foreign missionary. But whether as an individual, or as a group of individuals, *you* can be of tremendous help and blessing to those who are serving our Lord.

7

IDEAS FOR HELPING MISSIONARIES ON FURLOUGH

Now that we have considered some of the things we can do for our missionaries out on the field, we come to another situation where we can be of inestimable help to missionaries. This has to do with those who are presently in the States for furlough. Perhaps you will be able to enjoy a personal visit with your missionary during his time at home; or it may be that you have never had a personal part in providing for the needs of God's servants. There is so much that can be done that no one needs to feel that his part is unimportant or unnecessary. Individuals, groups, or whole churches can become involved.

Let's consider first some of those things that can help give missionaries on furlough a warm welcome home, to allow them a certain amount of normalcy in their busy lives, and to help prepare them for eventual return to their field of service.

HOUSEHOLD ITEMS

At the top of the list in the minds of missionaries who will be in the States only temporarily is household items. Most of their earthly goods are stored or being used by others on the field during their absence. It would be impossible for them to store sufficient items in the States to make a comfortable housing situation each time they come home. It would also be unwise to transport their necessary living items from the field for furlough.

Thus, the missionary arrives home with a few well-worn clothes, some souvenirs, slides of his work, and little else. Almost immediately, he is faced with a need for cooking utensils, dishes, linens, and furniture. Most of us have more than we need of all of these items. Is it possible that you have some pots and pans, or an old but still usable set of dishes? Plastic dishes can now be purchased fairly inexpensively. They are pretty and durable. A gift set would be useful for furlough duty and then could be taken to the field. Why not stock up on towels, sheets, pillowcases, tablecloths, napkins, and/or bedspreads at the semiannual white sales? These are all essential items for setting up housekeeping. Let the missionary know if they are only for his furlough use or if they are his to keep, in which case, he may take them back to the field. (So make sure they are of good quality.) If your missionary settles in your area, you and your friends will probably be able to provide pieces of furniture. If he settles elsewhere, you could send a money gift to help with this expense.

Appliances, both small and large (including a washing machine, sewing machine, refrigerator, radio, toaster), will be a real source of pleasure. If you are considering giving an appliance, try to find out exactly what would be most useful, and what might be of use if he were to take it back to the field with him. You can still loan him these things if he can't take them back to the field.

A clock is a useful gift. If it is only to be used at home, an electric or battery-operated timepiece is appropriate. If the missionary is the new owner of the clock, he might well prefer a travel or regular wind-up alarm clock. These will be useful on the field as well as in the States.

We have almost forgotten about the days when all we had for cleaning our rugs was a lowly carpet sweeper. In our sophistication, we now use vacuum sweepers. There are still many places in the world, however, where electricity is non-existent, and a carpet sweeper would be a blessing. Since it would be difficult to send through the mail, give it to your missionary on furlough so he can use it here and take it back with him.

All types of kitchenware can be used during furlough days. An eggbeater, potato masher, measuring cups and spoons, spatula, sharp knives, mixing bowls, refrigerator dishes, and rolling pin will please any homemaker.

HOSPITALITY

High on your list of priorities for helping missionaries on furlough should be the intangible necessity of hospitality.

Most missionaries are required to travel extensively during their time in the States. Perhaps you are about to purchase a new car. Why not give the missionary your trade-in, if it is in good condition? Or perhaps you have an extra car which you could loan your missionary during furlough.

If your missionary prefers to use public transportation, why not send a special gift of money to help cover this expense? If he is to come to your area to speak at your church, you will certainly want to provide his round-trip ticket.

It is becoming increasingly difficult for missionaries to find suitable housing when they come to the States. In some instances, they are here for only three months. If their family can put them up, there is no problem, but many times this is not a possibility. You may have an apartment or home which missionaries could occupy during their furlough period. They are willing to pay rent, of course. If you cannot provide a "permanent" temporary abode, do consider providing housing during your annual missionary conference or when your missionary (and his family) are able to visit. Some churches have been very careful to provide housing units for their church missionaries either at no cost or at very low rates. The usual problems missionaries face include the location of a suitable dwelling, the tremendously high rent charged in most places, and the problem of having to sign a lease for a period of one year, which may not fit into the furlough schedule.

When a missionary family is in your area, why not volunteer for some free babysitting? (This could include young children, too.) It is often difficult for missionaries to keep up a heavy schedule of meetings, especially during missionary conferences, and still give the proper care and attention to the younger members of their family. Most churches have adequate nursery facilities, but the nursery is not always open for prayer meeting or young people's services. This means that the missionary must be responsible for his children during those hours. You could bring much joy to that family by taking care of those children at these odd hours. It will help you to become better acquainted with them also.

If a missionary is staying in your home, one of the nicest things you could do is give him the use of your telephone. This is especially important if he has just arrived from the field and longs to say hello to a dear one, his family, his pastor, or a close friend on the other side of the country. It is also important if he is just about to return to the field and would like one last fond farewell with someone special. Perhaps he is traveling alone on deputation work and misses his family. A missionary usually feels that telephone calls are a luxury he cannot afford. Perhaps your church could make an unwritten rule that each missionary who visits may make up to three long-distance calls on the church phone. Or you, as an individual, may be willing to bear the cost for a call or two.

Also, if a missionary is staying in your home, loan him a key to your door. This will give him a feeling of independence and "homeliness." Many times, missionaries feel they are forced into a mold when they are guests in a supporter's home. Allow him some freedom, some quiet time, some fun, some self-reliance. Such kindness will never be forgotten.

If a missionary has never visited in your area, or has never seen some of the interesting places nearby, why not take him *sight-seeing?* It is better not to plan jaunts of this type without the knowledge and permission of your guest. But it is very possible he would enjoy a visit to Bunker Hill and Plymouth Rock if he is in Boston, a trip to the Seaquarium and the Parrot Jungle if he is in Miami, a ride on a cable car and a bus ride to the Japanese Gardens if he is in San Francisco, or a walk through the flower gardens and a picnic by the river in Ruralsville, U.S.A. If his children are along, why not ask permission to take them to the local zoo, a museum, the planetarium, or other local attractions. This will allow the parents a few hours of rest or a time of being alone together, which occurs all too seldom for busy missionaries on furlough.

If a missionary decides to stay in your area for any length of time, be sure to make him feel welcome within your church. He needs a church home. It may not be possible for him to settle in the area where he maintains membership; or perhaps there have been problems in his home church during his time on the field, and he is no longer part of its ministry. In any case, it is important that he put down roots in a place where he can join in work and worship with those of like precious faith. In some situations, it may be possible to offer him an associate membership in your church while he retains his membership elsewhere. (Some missionaries are required to maintain full membership in their supporting church or the church of which they are a member in order to continue to receive support funds from that organization. Therefore, some missionaries cannot be persuaded, under any circumstances, to give up that membership, even though they may be hundreds of miles distant and spend very little time with those people during furlough.)

Did you ever think of offering a missionary a job? True, he is usually busily engaged in meetings, travel, and family responsibilities. He still may want a job for various reasons.

Think of the missionary who has found it necessary to build schools and hospitals and houses on the mission field, with no formal training in this area. Perhaps you are in construction. Why not offer some on-the-job training? Perhaps the missionary is an engineer, and he would like to be updated in his field. You may be in a position to employ him for a while to help him adjust to changing and challenging ideas.

Your missionary may be a nurse who has not considered nursing in the States because she knows nothing about the new drugs and machines in use today, and she is afraid to walk into the personnel office of a modern hospital. Perhaps you could introduce her to the director of nurses, or the in-service director of your local hospital where she may be able to gain invaluable experience through refresher courses and orientation classes plus actual nursing practice.

Many jobs can be done by missionaries. The experience they could gain would be of great help and personal satisfaction to all involved. Consider this possibility. And don't forget: they need the money too!

If your missionary is a member of your church, or would be willing to join the group of local believers, and if he does not have to travel long distances every few days, it might be of benefit to him and to the church as a whole if he were to be appointed visitation pastor, or minister of youth during his furlough.

Why not offer your missionaries a free holiday? A week at a Bible conference to refresh their spirits, or a week at the seashore or in the mountains with no work responsibilities, will do more to rehabilitate weary workers than you can imagine. Most mission boards insist that their missionaries have a time for rest and recreation upon their return to the States. You can help in that regard. You may even have a little cabin at the lake, which you could allow them to use for a week or two.

When your missionary visits, why not have an open house for him? This will mean opening your home and allowing your friends and neighbors to visit in an informal way with him. In such an informal atmosphere, everyone seems much more human than he does at church! Not only so, but neighbors will often drop by to see pictures of Africa when they would turn down a cup of coffee and your personal witness. Do prepare your missionary in advance for this event, though. It should not be a surprise party (unless it is a surprise shower, when people have been asked to bring items of equipment and other goods).

Another thing that the term *hospitality* suggests is food. When he is on the field, your missionary would probably enjoy a food package filled with some of the special things he is unable to obtain in that country. It is a good idea to ask him about this when he visits you, for while he is in the homeland setting, he will better remember the things he sometimes craves but cannot get "out there." Even while he is home, he may not be able to get some of the things he craves, not because they are unavailable but simply because they are too expensive. A family from the Dominican Republic recently told us that they can afford to eat meat only twice a week here in the States. If your missionary is staying with you, give him some good meals, either in your home or in a restaurant. Allow him to have whatever he wants on the menu. (Many folks will order chopped beef whether they really like it or not, simply because it is usually less expensive than other dishes.) On the other hand, don't insist on going to the most expensive eating place and ordering a large sirloin if your friends would enjoy some tasty fried chicken.

Your missionary will not always be close enough for you to cook him a meal or take him out to eat. A parcel containing a cake, some cookies, or fudge can be sent to him. A package of tinned and packaged goods will always be appreciated. A

special money gift designated for an anniversary dinner, birthday party for the children, or "just for something you've
wanted" will be a morale booster.

You may also wish to show your hospitality by offering
your missionary the opportunity to take advantage of certain
bargains. If you own a store or a business, you may be able to
offer a discount on some very necessary items or pieces of
equipment which your missionary may need. Perhaps you
know of bargain stores in your area with which your missionary is not acquainted, or you have heard of a store which is
going out of business: share the information with your missionary. You may be helping him to obtain things he needs
but could not, under ordinary circumstances, afford.

EQUIPMENT

Along this line, also, there are times when very large pieces
of equipment become available to the public at auction, at
cost, or as gifts. These could include such things as power
plants, x-ray and other medical equipment, small calculators,
bookkeeping machines, typewriters, television cameras and
equipment, telephones, cloth, and more. Almost every mission board has had the experience of having one or more of
these items donated to them. No one will ever realize what
has been accomplished with such surplus or outdated items.
Keep your missionary's work in mind if you hear of any such
items becoming available. If you do not know too much
about the scope of the work done by the board to which your
missionary belongs, be sure to notify him of any equipment
which might be made available and let him have first refusal
on it.

Other things we should include with equipment are drugs,
which you might acquire through your personal physician
who throws away hundreds of dollars' worth of samples in a
year; replacement parts for any piece of equipment presently
owned by the missionary; audiovisual equipment, including

slide projectors, movie projectors, filmstrips and projectors for their use, overhead projectors, 16-mm sound films; a mobile unit which can be set up for distributing medicine or for evangelistic services. No missionary should be without a typewriter with plenty of extra ribbons.

All of these items should be made available to the missionary on furlough, for it is far better for him to arrange for shipping such things to the field when he is here than your trying to get them into his country after he has reached it. Then too it is possible that he already has some of this equipment. Check with him before purchasing any large item. If he needs it, be sure he shares certain specifications with you. Some audiovisual equipment may have to be gas-powered, or he may have to run it off the battery in his jeep. Other electrical equipment will have to be run with the use of a transformer. Missionaries will almost always prefer manual over electric typewriters. So if you have something on hand, offer it to your missionary, but if it must be purchased, let him tell you exactly what he needs.

CHILDREN'S NEEDS

Don't forget the children of your missionaries. Offer to give them games, dolls, stuffed animals, toys. Then, too, some missionary children have lived in handed-down clothing their entire lives. Some things fit them and others did not. Clothing and shoes for growing children can be expensive. Are your girls grown up and married? Perhaps you could spare one of their dolls for a missionary child who has never owned one. Perhaps some of their clothing still hangs in a closet. Offer them to the missionary parent. Some of you will want to take the children to a store and buy them something new and all their very own.

I once heard of a fourteen-year-old missionary daughter who cried for hours for joy after she was allowed to go to a store and pick out a dress. It was the first time in her life she had had this privilege. Not all missionary children have lived out of the missionary barrel, but you will not embarrass a child by either buying or making clothing which is especially for him or her.

EXPENSES

Expenses for professional services can be a missionary's financial undoing. Most mission boards make good provision for times of illness when hospital care is needed. But too often the missionary on furlough finds he is running up large medical bills for things not covered by insurance, such as measles, mumps, chicken pox, shots and vaccinations necessary for return to the field, or psychological counseling for one of the family. Then there is the cost of dental care.

Although most foreign countries today have more adequate medical facilities than ever before, dental care is still at a premium. Therefore, when missionaries come home, they feel it is essential to have a dental checkup. Today, dentists are interested not only in pulling or filling teeth, they are keenly interested in saving every possible tooth. Partial plates, bridgework, gold inlays, capping, plus X rays, cleaning, fillings, and perhaps some root canal work are suggested. Children often are sent to an orthodontist for braces or other equipment. Friends of mine recently returned to the field with a $3,000 debt in their account just from dental expenses incurred while they were home.

A visit to the eye doctor should be part of the routine for a missionary on furlough. Quite often, glasses will be prescribed, if only for reading ease. Because the prescription is difficult to have filled overseas, usually two pairs of glasses are purchased. Or prescription sunglasses may be essential.

Legal help may also be needed during furlough. Wills should be made out or updated. Power of attorney should be granted to someone in the States so that necessary business can be attended to without delay.

Missionaries certainly do not expect their supporters to bear all of their personal expenses for them. But having faced some of these costs yourself, you will readily understand that on the limited income received by most missionaries, these unexpected or extra expenses can cause severe hardships. The missionary may have to take on extra work in order to pay his debts. He may even have to retire from missionary work. Mission boards do not look favorably upon missionaries returning to the field with large debts in their account, unless there is the prospect of these bills being cleared up by those who will pledge to help in this regard.

Perhaps you are in the professional field and could offer your missionary your services free or at a discount. (It can also be taken as a deduction for income tax purposes.) Or you may wish to give a cash gift through the mission board for a particular need in the medical, legal, or dental area.

PERSONAL ITEMS

If you come to know a missionary to a greater extent than that you recognize him when he visits your church, you may wish to provide him with more than a check in the offering plate once a month. He will appreciate your personal interest in him and will be glad for any of the following items or others you may think of.

Every missionary should have a camera. If he has one already, he may need a newer model or replacement. You may have one you don't use or need. Offer it to him.

Clothing which you have on hand in good condition, in his size, and not outdated, can be offered, or new clothes can be purchased. You may have other clothing which he may be able to give to nationals on his station. Ask him about this.

Many missionaries would take correspondence or other educational courses, if they knew of them and received some financial help for them. Many home study courses are inexpensive and exceedingly helpful. Courses at community colleges, high schools, or at business establishments might be just what the missionary needs to update his knowledge and skills. Appraise him of their availability. Perhaps you could help him with the expense.

Does your missionary family have a new baby? You could become very popular with them by providing a supply of disposable diapers. These would be especially convenient for those who must travel almost constantly and find that the family must go along.

Missionary ladies and daughters very seldom have a good selection of jewelry. They may not often wear it on the field, but it is usually appropriate in the States. Do you have some that you no longer wear? Bracelets, necklaces, pins? What lovely gifts they make!

On the field, the missionary often lives with bars on his windows and locks on everything else. This necessitates carrying a number of keys wherever he goes. Why not give him a key case or key ring as a reminder of your care for him every time he opens a lock?

Have you ever seen a missionary leave for the field? He will almost always be standing in the midst of several suitcases and footlockers. Unless he is going out for the first time, some of the suitcases may be scuffed, broken, or held together with rope. Why not donate a new suitcase or footlocker? Missionaries need something light but durable, since most of them now fly to their destination. They need something practical for furlough use and something to store things in on the field. Although a beautiful matched set of luggage is always a lovely gift, missionaries are grateful even for unmatched items, as long as they will serve their purpose.

A wallet or purse is an acceptable contribution. Most of us manage to use these just about every day of our lives!

If you really want your missionary to think of you and remember your interest in him, give him a watch. This does not have to be 24-karat gold filled, surrounded by diamonds, or a family heirloom. A shockproof, waterproof, readable watch is the most practical. It should be constructed to take a good deal of wear and tear and still keep accurate time, but it does not have to be expensive or ornate. You can be sure your missionary will look at your gift many times in the course of a day.

Two more items make ideal gifts for any missionary. These are cash and a credit card. There seems little need to stress further how much your missionary needs every dollar you can share with him. A word needs to be said for credit cards. Nearly every store and gasoline company issues credit cards. Why not loan a card to your missionary with or without restrictions as to use (depending on how well you know him). It may prove to be more expensive than you thought (sacrifices of love often are), if you loan your gasoline credit card to a missionary for a month or two! I mentioned the possibility of loaning a card when I spoke at a meeting in a church which gives over a quarter of a million dollars annually to missions. Several men came to me afterward to thank me, saying it was a way they could become involved, and that it had not occurred to them before.

The home or local church should offer to provide for the missionary a commissioning service, or in the case of returning missionaries, a recommissioning service. At this service, the missionary is allowed to rededicate his life to the Lord for His work. Often, other missionaries from his board who may be in the area or representatives from the board itself, are invited to attend and take part in the service. It can be a time of encouragement to your missionary and an inspiration to the entire congregation.

ATTITUDES

Certain attitudes should be shared with missionaries on furlough. They should have your confidence and friendship. They should sense a spirit of optimism, encouragement, and enthusiasm. No downgrading of missionary work as a profession, please. Mediocrity is lukewarmness. Halfheartedness promotes disinterest. It is essential that you be either hot or cold. Your zeal, zip, and zest should be an inspiration to your missionary. Your own eager interest and enthusiasm will go a long way toward making your missionary a better worker. When an individual gets the feeling that no one really cares, his work suffers. A friend of mine used to ask one of her employees how he was doing. Each day, he would answer, "Just barely!" Nothing will dishearten your missionary more than seeing you doing "just barely." Live a little, show a bit of spunk, and take some action. Share with him what you and others in your church are doing for the Lord. He is interested in knowing that.

Share information which may be of benefit. He may have been away from the country for three, four, or five years. He will appreciate being updated on trends and topics.

Your own patriotism will be appreciated. You may feel that things have not gone too well in some areas of politics and practice. But America is still highly blessed of God, and your missionary is glad to be on home soil. Tears come to his eyes when he sees the Stars and Stripes flying in the breeze. Encourage him that he can still be proud of his country.

Has your individual or church support of a missionary been confined to financial donations for his ministry? Are you beginning to see that support can be personalized to a greater extent? Putting your cash or check in the missionary offering is commendable, but perhaps you are thinking you would like to do more. I have mentioned in this chapter a number of things which can be given to your missionary to strengthen the cause of missions. Some of the items are distinctly for his pleasure and use during furlough. Some will be used during furlough and then taken to the field for additional use.

It should be pointed out that friendship is as important

to your missionary as anything else you can give to him. And as you take a deeper interest in him, you may be able to lead others to do likewise. It is possible that you could move your entire church to become more fully involved in missions and missionaries.

It should also be mentioned that you will not be able to do everything mentioned here for every missionary who comes your way. But do what you can. Others will be able to supply other needs. As a result, your missionary will be better treated in the future than he has been in the past, for you are now aware of some of the ways in which you can enter into partnership with him.

I have not meant to imply that missonaries are paupers and that they have few resources as far as earthly goods are concerned. This is not true. Neither did I intend to create the impression that missionaries are not willing and able to buy those things that are necessary for them to carry out meaningful activities, or that they are unwilling to provide for their own family. But as we take a practical look at the missionary, we see one who is utterly dependent upon God to supply his needs through individuals whom He enables to do so. Missionaries, in most cases, live within restricted budgets. Their salary is based upon their needs in their field of service. This means that when they are on furlough, though most receive an increased support allotment for those months, it is difficult for them to budget those funds in order to cover the complete costs of food, housing, travel, education, and equipment necessary for return to the field. So, I am suggesting that you can have a vital part in making these items available to your missionary. It may be by providing dollars. It may be by the loan or gift of household items. It may be by providing professional services at cost. It may be by sharing information which will result in money saved by the missionary. He is not helpless and poverty stricken, but your partnership with him in these matters will serve not only to provide his needs, but will result in blessing to you in your fellowship of sharing. If God allows you the privilege of providing for His people, take advantage of it.

8

WHAT *NOT* TO GIVE YOUR MISSIONARY

In the last chapter, I suggested a number of things that you can do to help your missionary. Now let us consider some of those things you may give that will hinder rather than help your missionary. Furlough time can be frustrating or full of joy and times of growth and encouragement. *You* can make the difference! Many of the prohibitions we shall list would be profitable for all Christians to apply to their relationships with other people. But they apply very specifically to your relationship with those who serve the Lord as missionaries. Since it would be difficult to indicate those matters which are of most or least importance, we shall simply list our don'ts in alphabetical order.

Among the things which are best not given to missionaries are the following:

ENDLESS LARGE MEALS

The human body requires certain foods and liquids to maintain itself. But three huge meals and two or three large snacks during a day can make your missionary fat, lazy, and/or ill. If he is visiting a different home for each meal, each family will want to serve him the best they have. If possible, check with others who will honor him as their guest on "your" day. Work out your menus in such a way that you can feed your missionary sensibly—showing true care and concern!

JUNK

When an item serves no useful purpose, or is too worn to be acceptable to your associates, or you want a new one for yourself, the servant of God is very apt to be the recipient of your possession. Put your junk in the garbage can. Give your missionary only what is equal in wearability and quality to what you would accept for your own use.

PETS

If your missionary family arrives at your home just after the kittens, don't do them the favor of giving their children those tiny fluffs of fur, not without first asking them privately. Pets are wonderful to have, but four kittens and three children in the station wagon during furlough can be hectic! If the children are settled nearby and the family will not be moving about, they may welcome your gift. But be sure to ask and receive permission before being too generous.

WORLDLY PLEASURES

Many events are coming up. The symphony is too good to be missed. The stock car races are on. You just happen to have an extra ticket for the football game. Now your missionary is due for a visit. What happens to all your plans? This can be a ticklish question. You may attend all such events without thoughts pro or con. But your missionary will, in many cases, have second thoughts about some of these things. He may object. Therefore, never include him in your plans until you have checked with him in advance. Don't feel rejected or hurt if he refuses your invitation. There may be certain places and events which he does not or cannot attend because of personal conviction. He will not hinder you from going, but in the same spirit, do not force *him* to attend.

Apart from these things which should not be given without a missionary's full knowledge and consent, there are attitudes which should have no part in your relationship with him.

ABANDONMENT

Don't forget your missionary when he leaves your church, your home, or your country. Maintain some kind of communication with him. If you decide to stop supporting him because, for unforeseen circumstances, you are not able to continue your part in his ministry, be honest with him. Don't let him return to the field thinking he has your continuing financial support if, in reality, he does not. This puts him in a very difficult situation. On the other hand, if you share this information with him while he is at home or with you, he is able to find another supporter to supply the amount he needs.

ACCUSATIONS

General statements made in the presence of others concerning what you think your missionary is or should be, has done or could be doing with his time and money, are out of place. If you discover firsthand, without denial, that your missionary is not worthy of your investment, tell him directly and settle with him. But do not accuse him of things behind his back which may be true or false, or a matter of misunderstanding or misinformation.

ANXIETY

Don't share only bad or pessimistic news. Don't use your support as pressure to make him engage in what you think his ministry ought to be. Make your relationship one of true fellowship and joy so that your missionary doesn't have to weigh every word and action in order to try to keep your interest.

APATHY

This is, undoubtedly, one of the most devastating attitudes possible. It produces lethargy, disinterest, and stagnation. Be *for* your missionary, or *against* him. Don't just tolerate him. Don't listen without some type of reaction. Apathy will destroy not only your own missionary vision and service, but will tend to render your associates apathetic also. Whole missionary programs have been destroyed or rendered inoperative because of apathy. Your missionary should be allowed to become a very real member of your fellowship and society. Don't relegate him to the position of a lower class individual, a poor man with no resources, a man begging for support. He must be one with you. Making him other than an integral part of your fellowship is unwarranted. Every living person needs to be noticed. Care for your missionary. Listen to him. He doesn't want sympathy; he merely wants to know that you realize he exists. If your missionary is speaking at your church or in your area, unless you are physically unable to attend his meeting, don't stay home and expect him to come to you.

ARGUMENTS

Some people take pride in opposing everything and everybody. You may want to argue your view of the politics of the country your missionary works in or the policies of his board. Exchange of ideas and communication of thoughts is stimulating, but arguments only produce hard feelings. Also, unless you have lived where he is living, you have, at best, only a vicarious experience of all that he faces. He is probably right, after all!

ATTITUDE OF SUPERIORITY

Because you have stayed at home and have become "successful," have obtained the best possible education, and are the means of financial support for your missionary, does not make you greater than he. Only one who has humbled himself to accept all that he has from others will fully understand how the missionary feels. Yet, what do any of us have that we have not received from others? And what do any of us possess that has not been loaned to us by our Lord Himself?

BARRENNESS

Missionaries give out spiritual food to such an extent in their service that they often return home starved. Help them to be fed. Don't deny them the privilege of regaining spiritual stamina. Don't expect them to speak at every meeting they attend. Allow them to take in as well as give out. You can be a source of spiritual help. Be sure that your spiritual life is not barren and unfruitful. Barren Christians can be of little help to others.

BIGOTRY

Bigots are being laughed at these days because they have been shown in a humorous light on certain television shows. But real-life bigots are not appreciated. Many of our missionaries work among races and ethnic groups about whom we are conditioned to be bigoted. Squelch the temptation to reveal your personal feelings about these people, unless you confess it privately and ask for enlightenment to help you overcome these feelings.

BITTERNESS

Your own personal disappointments should not become a burden to your missionary. If you feel that someone, the church, or something has wronged you and you are holding a grudge, don't transfer this bitterness to God's servant. He may already have reasons for being bitter. Try to be a help to him.

BOREDOM

This, perhaps, is an outgrowth of apathy. If you are bored with missions, try to do something about it, but don't transfer your feelings to the man who needs your interest. If he is a guest in your home, don't barrage him with what *you* say and do and are. Give him a chance, too. And please don't entertain him with the television set for eighteen hours a day.

CASUAL INTEREST

If you are not truly willing to be a missionary supporter without some big *if's* attached, settle it in your own heart. Don't place the burden for your interest entirely on your missionary. Meet him at least part way.

CONCEIT

Your missionary is a human being. He needs encouragement, but don't overdo it to the extent that he becomes conceited and begins to think of himself and his profession more highly than he ought to think. He has probably sacrificed little more than a number of the people in your congregation who faithfully support him. His work is a team effort. No man can do it by himself. Putting your missionary on a pedestal is bad for all parties concerned. It's embarrassing, unnecessary, and uncalled for. Love him, support him, but don't worship him.

No missionary was ever an angel! Don't expect him to act like those specially created creatures just because of the importance you have placed upon him.

Missionaries are like grapes—just one of the bunch. They want no special favors. They request no special treatment. They want to fit into your plans and programs to the best of their ability.

COOL RECEPTION

When your missionary visits, give him a warm welcome. If he feels like an uninvited guest, he will have due cause to question your interest in him and the work he represents. Don't be passive. Ask questions. Learn all you can from your missionary.

CRITICISM

What you think of your pastor, church, neighbors, and friends does not need to be shared in all its fullness with your missionary; and if you have something against him, criticize him privately and personally in the love of Christ—never in public.

DECEIT

Don't make your missionary think you are something you are not. Don't use the editorial *we* for boasting about your Christian charity and works unless you have been personally engaged in the ministries of which you speak. How easy it is for someone in the congregation to state, "We provide services for the Rescue Mission, three convalescent homes, and a hospital; we go out on visitation twice each week; we provide home study courses for shut-ins; we sing at four services each week," and so on. Just tell him what *you* do.

Be real clear through. Don't put on a front of spirituality. If you don't have it, don't try to impress the missionary that you do. Take stock of yourself in this matter, but don't cover up the lacks in your life by using all the religious jargon.

Don't make a big deal out of the appearance of your missionary and then relegate him to the archives of the church calendar until the next time he appears. This amounts to little more than ministerial pomp and circumstance. Perhaps you feel you must be extremely spiritual where it concerns your missionary. Not so. Be yourself! Be normal and natural. He will appreciate this balance.

DETACHMENT

Your missionary is a part of the Christian community. He needs to have a sense of belonging. Don't put him in a corner and a category by himself. Don't stay aloof. Show your consideration. One of the best gifts you can give is understanding. There are times when this will be difficult. But as it has been so truly stated, understanding is a large part of loving. Your missionary may have good reasons for being out of fashion, independent, impatient, or seemingly unique.

DISCONTINUED INTEREST

Since your missionary last visited, you have decided to support an orphange instead of him. Therefore, when he arrives on the scene, you treat him in a cool and unfriendly manner. But remember, money is not the only thing you can give. Continue to maintain an interest in him and his work even if you no longer support it with your finances. You can still invite him to your home. You can still be his friend. If he feels like talking, listen. (Too many people today listen to friends with one ear and the TV with the other.)

DISCOURAGEMENT AND DISAPPOINTMENT

These are the last things God's people need. Bolster your missionary's morale. Don't destroy it. Did you realize missionaries expect something from you other than your money and prayers? They desire God's best for you. They pray that you will have a ministry, that you will live a life well-pleasing to the Lord, that you will maintain a witness which will be a light in your community. Don't let them down.

EXCUSES

Have you found yourself trying to explain why you didn't give or pray or write? Or why you aren't involved in Christian causes? Such excuses can become tedious. Save them for someone else, and resolve not to have to make excuses in the future.

EXHAUSTION

Give your fellow Christian a break. Let him rest. If he wants to do nothing, let him do it. And when he is on the field, don't demand that he work tirelessly all hours of the day and night.

FEARS

Your attitude toward your country, your government, your young people, your peers, and your church will have an effect upon your missionary. He may have qualms anyway about having to leave his children in schools here, so don't encourage him to worry. Or, if you know he is petrified when he speaks to a group of people, don't inform him that the richest man in town will be attending his service and is ready to donate a new wing for the mission hospital *if* the speaker impresses him.

FEELINGS OF HELPLESSNESS AND HOPELESSNESS

Experience on the field makes God's servants independent in their work. Be kind and helpful, and don't ever hold the attitude that you are the only one who can do things right. When a missionary family visits you, let them help with the duties you would normally allow a friend to do. Then too, missionaries go forth with the impossible dream, "It can be done." And they usually accomplish what they set out to do. Don't try to convince them that their task is impossible.

GREED

You obviously have had your needs met. Don't impress your missionary with how nice it would be for him to enter the business or professional world at home and make a splendid living for himself and his family. Don't try to force him to reconsider his calling from God merely to seek prestige, titles, money, or fame.

GRIEF AND GLOOM

Did you know that your missionary is concerned for you? Don't cause him grief through your attitudes or actions. He expects you to be as spiritually mature as you expect him to be. There is nothing worse than visiting friends at a funeral parlor! If problems are causing you to be gloomy much of the time, postpone a long visit until you can be your natural, positive self. Remember that your depressed mood will linger in your friend's mind long after the visit. Gloom usually spells defeat. No one needs it!

INCONSISTENCY

Provide some stability for your missionary friend. Don't be for his work one minute and against it the next. Don't accept him today and reject him tomorrow. Don't flatter him now and deny him later.

INFERIORITY COMPLEX

No, the missionary is not super special. But neither is he inferior to his peers in other professions or lines of work. Treat him as an equal.

JESTS

There are jokes galore about missionary service. But remarks which hit the missionary below the belt or show him in an unfavorable light, are both unfair and uncalled for. They are unhealthy for the speaker as well as for the one at whom the poke is aimed.

Your missionary deserves the best that your mind, spirit, prayers, and money can provide. Don't share only the fluff of life with him. Having fellowship means more than telling one joke after the other.

LEFT-HANDED COMPLIMENTS

Don't beat around the proverbial bush in expressing appreciation. Be forthright and positive. Let your missionary know you really mean it (but only if you do, of course).

MEAGER ALLOWANCE

Life does not consist in the abundance of things one has. But there are certain necessities for everyday living which are required by all. Don't cause your missionary to waste his time, energy, and spiritual power in begging God for his daily bread when you could easily supply that need.

NAGGING AND NOSINESS

Don't pester your missionary with personal questions, and demand answers concerning mission practices. If you are truly interested, ask questions. But don't pry into those areas the missionary does not care to talk about, especially family problems or other personal areas, unless you are directly involved or he wants to share them with you. A meddlesome and officious supporter can turn a missionary's hair white overnight. Even if your missionary is willing to answer questions, don't wear him out by asking trivial and unanswerable questions which have little or no importance for you. The end result should be a better understanding of the missionary and his problems.

NOISE

Fun and laughter are fine. But lively entertainment is not always the best choice for a tired missionary. Most missionaries appreciate a time when they don't have to speak, go, see, do, be. Get out of the house and let him do what he wants for a few hours, or let him get out and walk or sit or think or play the piano.

When your missionary is in a church service where he has no speaking responsibilities, don't disrupt this worship ex-

perience by whispering, talking, or laughing during the pre-
lude, solo, offering, or message. Not only your missionary,
but all those seated in your vicinity will be most grateful.

PASTORAL RESPONSIBILITIES

A pastor is called upon to perform many duties. Some
duties are pleasant. Others are not. Don't save the most unpleasant ones for the missionary's visit, thinking he will be
able to handle the situation with no commitment. If you are
the pastor of the church, these are matters for you to handle.
If such things as tragedies occur while the missionary is physically present with you, you might invite him to go along to
counsel. But never leave your most difficult work for someone else to handle.

RITUALISM

Some churches go through a standard form when a missionary visits: a covered-dish supper, a prayer for his success, an opportunity for him to speak and introduce his family, and a corner by the door where he can greet exiting members. The
same two missionary hymns are sung at each gathering. An offering is taken after the slides are shown. Don't fall into such a
rut. Change your presentations. Change your hymns. Ask the
missionary to choose his favorite songs. Don't let this missionary service become a carbon copy of every preceding one.
This is one of the easiest ways to kill a missionary program in
the local church.

ROAST PASTOR AND PEOPLE

Some complaints are for family airing only. Rumors about
the church and its members are not public luncheon meat
for the missionary.

RUDENESS

This can be a personal thing, but it can also be broader

than that. Many a missionary has entered a service prepared to share his work, only to find that a "big name" has unexpectedly dropped into the sanctuary; after this individual has been introduced and asked to say a word and his wife has sung an unscheduled solo, the missionary is allowed the remaining ten minutes "to do anything you like." This type of situation is rudeness at its worst and should be avoided at any cost.

Missionaries on furlough often are heard to say, "I'll be glad to get back to the field to get some rest." A strange indictment, but true, unfortunately, because of the desire of people in the churches at home to possess the missionary for every service and meeting imaginable. He is asked to speak at an evening service. He has already spoken in two churches that day. But when he comes to you, he is asked to speak to the combined young people's groups, have refreshments with the career group, speak at the evening service, show slides afterward, and then speak and show slides at his host's home following the formal meetings. If this is what an evening can become, just think how easily you could kill your missionary with such kindness during an entire *week* of services!

SYMPATHY

God's workers do not want your sympathy. They want your love, your encouragement, and your prayers on their behalf. If they look for or accept sympathy, they are probably on their way to resigning from their board.

TENSION

Your missionary should feel that he is at home and among friends. It is your responsibility to see that he is. Before he arrives, don't send a confidential letter telling him that the new pastor seems less missions-minded than the former one. Or just before he speaks, don't casually mention that the mission board will be meeting after the service to decide whether to continue his support.

VULGARITY

From Christians? Unbelievable! No, quite possible. You are entertaining your missionary in your home, and for lack of anything better to do, you turn on the TV. A number of programs you may find quite amusing are considered out of taste and vulgar to your friend. Is he a goody-goody? No! He has lived where the delineation between what is sinful and what is wholesome is more pronounced. Perhaps where he is serving, the body is not exposed for the purpose of physical excitement or entertainment. Be very selective in the entertainment you choose for your missionary guest.

XENOPHOBIA

Many missionaries have it. Many others catch it. What is it? A fear of strangers or foreigners. They didn't have it on their field of service; they got it when they came to you and your church. Don't remain a stranger to them. A warm welcome will usually cure this phobia so that it is short-lived.

YOKE

Some supporting churches and individuals try to harness their missionaries, monopolize their time, tell them what to do, how to do it, or how it could have or should have been done. Don't put a burden upon your missionary by pressing him into your stereotype or by being jealous of his ministry. Give him freedom to be himself and to serve the Lord.

ZENANA

When I returned home from the mission field, I was very pleased to be able to converse freely once again with men and women of all ages. You see, in the Moslem land in which I served, I could work and talk only with women and children. You miss a great deal when you live in such a cloistered situation, not being able to share the knowledge and advice of half of the population. Thus, when your missionary comes, don't put him in a zenana situation where he speaks only to those of his own sex. Make sure he is able to share in the fellowship of the whole congregation. Often the wife speaks to the women; the husband speaks to the men. It would be far better if this were reversed, or if both spoke to the combined group. Don't always send the women off to speak with the children, either. If you do, the children will come to understand that missionary work is only for women.

We have at least scratched the surface of things that are not appropriate gifts and attitudes for your missionary. Please give this chapter your thoughtful consideration before shrugging it off with, "How could anyone be so thoughtless?" You would be surprised!

9

WHAT TO EXPECT FROM YOUR MISSIONARY

Perhaps you have begun to feel that missionaries are just a little lower than the angels, and that when they appear on the horizon, you must act a lot differently, and they have yet to make their first mistake.

Fortunately, this is not the case. Your missionary is clothed in flesh just as you are; he suffers the same torments, agonies, joys, and happinesses that you do; he also needed salvation as you once did; he seeks to serve God in full-time service. He is no more God's chosen vessel than you are; he is not necessarily more capable in his chosen field than any other person of the same profession who remains in the homeland. Foreign missionaries are no more dedicated to the Lord than home missionaries, or Christian layworkers in the States. Your missionary gets angry; loses his temper; becomes impatient; gets lonely, tired, irritable, and disappointed. The kind word, the ready witness, the willing worker don't just happen magically. For some, witnessing is extremely difficult. Your missionary may not always be happy with his work, his family, his colaborers, and his mission. He may sometimes even raise questions and be plagued with doubts. He may come to dislike every interruption; he gets tired of smiling; he gets depressed over financial difficulties and the lack of converts. He is amazed at his indifference to the needs of some, his ingratitude to others, and his overwhelming desire to seek fellowship among the missionaries rather than with the nationals; he frets over his lack of trust and a slight superiority complex, when he knows the nationals are on a par with him as brothers in Christ and intelligent human beings. He is disturbed by the seeming lack of answers to his prayers, his lack of time in the Book and on his knees, the coldness which is beginning to enshroud his very soul, replacing his compassion. He has begun to discover that being a missionary has not made him forever invulnerable to the attacks of the evil one, but that it has produced gaps in his defense, and the enemy of his soul has made inroads that he never dreamed possible. He remembers that he is merely a man trying to do the work of God, and he hopes with all his heart that you will understand this.

He doesn't want to be set on a pedestal. He knows he isn't worthy of it by himself. In many ways, he looks up to *you* because of your faithfulness in ministering; he may feel insecure in your presence because he is completely dependent upon your partnership in prayer, giving, and caring, to allow him the privilege of serving the Lord. He is lost for words when it comes to saying, "Thank you for your help." He tries not to feel that you expect more of him than he is capable of producing.

Expect your missionary, therefore, to be as human as you are. Don't force him into a spiritual hypochondria, where he begins to wonder if there is something wrong with him because he falls short of your expectations. Don't feel that because he is a missionary, he is duty bound to preach and teach twenty-four hours a day, seven days a week. Allow him to blow off steam as a safety precaution. Don't force him to bottle up his experiences and emotions because you will think less of him if he expresses bad feelings. If you are a concerned Christian, don't expect your missionary to be more dedicated than you are.

You should expect your missionary to keep in touch with you, to share his life and ministry as he might share the course of a business venture with a financial partner. He should thank you for all you do in his behalf. Ingratitude is certainly not a virtue in anyone.

You should expect your missionary to be interested in you as a person, to ask questions, to share experiences. He wants you for a friend. He needs those who are a link between the field and his homeland.

You can expect your missionary to have difficult problems to solve. He is not well. Should he come home? His father has suffered a stroke. Is he needed to make medical arrangements? A teenager does not fit into the school for missionary children. Should he return to the States until the children are grown? There are rumors of a coup in the country. Should he leave now to be sure of getting away safely? A national believer has fallen into sin. How should he be disciplined? These are only a few of the issues that your missionary may be facing. One of these may be the reason he hasn't written you a letter for over six months, even though you've kept in touch regularly.

You can expect that when he is home on furlough, if it can possibly be arranged, he will want to visit you. But please remember that his own relatives come first. When your missionary arrives home from his field, he will be anxious to visit his family. He will then hope to get a chance to rest, relax, and be himself. He will also need time to arrange slides and prepare deputation messages, or to make arrangements to enter a course of study. Expect a delay in his coming to you. Understand that he is trying to catch up with himself, assess his needs, and evaluate his term of ministry. He has nothing personal against you causing him to delay his visit.

Keep in mind that with three- and six-month furloughs becoming popular, a missionary supported by many churches may not be able to visit them all during one furlough. If you hardly know him and your support is minimal in proportion to other groups and individuals, he may not even be able to visit you personally. As much as he would like to visit, you may be a thousand miles from his next nearest contact, and unless you offer to pay his fare, he may not have sufficient funds for such a trip. It does not mean that he is not grateful for your giving. But he must set priorities in how best to spend his furlough time, money, and energy.

If your missionary happens to be a relative, he will probably be in your area for more than one Sunday. Don't line him up for speaking engagements the moment he arrives. Be considerate. Let him enjoy the services his first week at home. Give him time to recharge his spiritual battery, and he will be the better for it.

Expect your missionary to be weary after a term of service. Just accept it and help him to bounce back by letting him adjust gradually to the tremendous changes which have taken place during his absence, and don't add undue tensions by expecting him to be full of exciting tales or willing to listen to lengthy discussions.

Expect your missionary to look to you as an example of Christians in the homeland. Your influence and attitude can well set the tone of his entire future ministry.

Many missionaries feel they are not serving the Lord when they are on furlough. Perhaps this is because you expect them to stand in the pulpit, explain their work, and show slides of their ministry, and that is all. Expect your missionary to want to proclaim Christ in his meetings. Allow him to give an invitation, to ask for a response to the call for willing workers, to speak to children's classes where he can freely introduce them to Jesus Christ, as he does on the field. Expect him to want this kind of a ministry in addition to being asked a zillion questions about his mission field.

Expect your missionary to be polite enough to eat everything you set before him, but be kind enough not to set a feast every two or three hours!

When he is back on the field, you can expect there will come an occasion when he will need your help in a particular situation, such as obtaining a special kind of transistor for his radio, catalogues from various schools for his son to peruse, a refill for his pen, or a book of sermon outlines. If you expect he will have a special need during his term, offer to be of help, and he will feel much happier about causing you the trouble of getting it for him.

Expect your missionary to move around a lot on the field. Don't picture him as being stationary. Don't begrudge him two-month vacations when you get only two weeks. His living conditions may be quite different than yours, so expect him to be allowed the extra time. (Undoubtedly he is using the time for further language study, local witnessing, planning for the coming year's work, pastoring the church at the hill station, or counseling at a young people's camp in the cooler or drier climate.)

You can expect that in the days to come, your missionary will have to assume a teaching role and will not be as much personally involved in reaching the people. He will be training nationals who will, in turn, take over the responsibility of winning souls to Christ, and seeing that they are fed and that churches are established and maintained.

Expect that living expenses will continually increase for your missionary. His board may have to raise his minimum salary requirement. Help as much as possible in supplying these needs.

More than anything else, you can expect that your missionary is counting heavily upon you to uphold him in the work of his ministry. Don't let him down. Hold the ropes of prayer securely while he goes out to rescue souls. You have the easier but certainly just as important task!

> If you cannot go yourself to save them,
> There are those that you can send,
> Then with loving hearts stretched out to help them,
> Hold the ropes while they descend.
>
> ANONYMOUS

10

MISSIONARY PROJECTS

It would be impossible to list all the things we could do to provide items for missions and their workers. I will mention just a few to stimulate your thinking. You will be able to add to the list according to your own circumstances and the needs of the individuals and groups which you support. The following projects will require the combined efforts of all interested folks in the church.

CHRISTMAS IN OCTOBER

Many members of a church send Christmas cards to other members. In place of this custom, why not place a large poster-board Christmas tree in a conspicuous spot in the church, possibly near the main entrance? Members could then place in an envelope the money they would have spent for cards and postage, and leave it under the tree. Then they would write their names on the Christmas tree for all to see. The money would be equally divided among your church missionaries and sent as personal gifts for holiday extras. Those with children in the family will be especially grateful. You see, missionary wives cannot take in ironing, and missionary children cannot shovel driveways to earn just a little extra for a once-a-year special treat. But you can provide that joy for them quite easily.

GIFT BOXES

Although some countries charge excessive customs duty, thus prohibiting the receipt of the boxes you would like to send, there are many areas where boxes can still be sent. It is best to hear from your missionary concerning what he would really like to have or items he needs. Books and magazines can be sent duty free, so this is no problem. Foodstuffs will be appreciated. Mixes of all kinds are light and easy to send (cakes, brownies, pancakes, pie crust, puddings, pizza, macaroni, etc.). Meat tenderizer is a very practical gift! Plastic wrap, plastic bags, and aluminum cooking foil are appreciated. Stuff them into the box as packing. Don't send items in bottles or other breakable containers. If soap or mothballs are sent, wrap them heavily and securely in foil so they do not flavor packaged foods.

A small toy for each child will be received with exceptional gratitude.

Paper napkins, clothespins, birthday candles, everyday cards, thread, needles, pins, pencils and pens, stationery, paper clips, and other small and common items are apt to be quite uncommon and difficult to obtain where your missionary is located. Check with your local post office concerning maximum measurements and weight for the countries to which you will send parcels. Consult the previous chapters for other ideas.

Either the members of the group can bring money toward the purchase of several items, or each person could bring an individual gift.

PROVIDING PROFESSIONAL AND BUSINESS SERVICES

Most churches have within their membership one or more doctors, nurses, lawyers, dentists, store owners, car salesmen, gas station operators, secretaries, photographers, printers, bankers, and other businessmen. It would be a fine offer to hand your missionary a list of all services members of the church could provide. Have you asked your missionary if he needs to open a checking account, has teeth in need of attention, requires shots before return to the field, needs pictures taken for the home office, would like his form letters or prayer cards printed, or needs a tankful of gas and a spare tire? Even nonprofessionals can donate the money toward these very needful expenses.

ITEM PROJECTS

Find out something your missionary or his board needs to carry on a more effective ministry. It may be a typewriter, projector, vehicle, visual aid, tape recorder, musical instrument, adding machine, piece of hospital equipment, or printing press. A church in the east even provided an airplane for a missionary organization.

HELPING MISSIONARY KIDS

Missionary children usually leave their parents and return to the homeland for college or work. Some must return for high school. Your church has the privilege of providing them with some of the things they need. Someone may be able to provide rent-free or low-rent lodging. Everyone can help them to become a part of your church family and make them feel at home at your regular and special events. The church may want to set up a scholarship fund to help them through college. Many churches have a testimony time during Sunday school when an individual praises God for some special blessing and places a special offering in a bank. Why not use the funds in that bank to provide spending money for your local MKs, or send it to a different one each month?

MISSIONARY SHOWER

Before a candidate leaves for his field of service (whether as a new recruit or as a returning missionary) why not provide a personal or general shower? There is no limit to the types of things you can provide. Ask your missionary for a list of specific items he still needs. This can be used as a guide for those who will participate. If it is a personal shower, be sure to ask for the necessary sizes.

VOLUNTEER WORK

Do you support an organization with an office in your area? Why not volunteer to help them get out a special mailing, or type form letters, or prepare material for the printer? A call to the director may provide you with much opportunity to be of service and have a more personal part in their ministry. A group could spend all day with a service project, saving the organization much time or money.

USED GREETING CARDS

In many areas, missionaries use the pictures from old greeting cards as attendance awards and for memory work prizes. Check with your missionary concerning the practicality of sending cards. If they cannot be used as awards, there are other possibilities. Carefully cut out the center section (which usually contains the actual greeting and personal salutations), leaving the front picture attached to the blank back section. They can then be used again as notepaper. Some missionaries who cannot obtain greeting cards prefer to receive the whole card with only the signature cut off so they can reuse it with its original sentiment. Pictures from greeting cards can be pasted on thin poster board or construction paper to make attractive bookmarks. Magazine pictures can also be utilized for this purpose. (Rubber cement works better with thin paper than paste or mucilage do.)

CLOTHING FOR YOUR MISSIONARY FAMILY

If you have a monthly women's missionary meeting, why not make a project of making clothing for the family to be taken to their field of service or to be used when they arrive home for furlough? Most missionaries do some pretty serious gulping when they look at the price tags on clothing in the homeland (don't we all?)! Purchasing material and making clothing, for those who have this practical and useful gift, is a contribution worth far more than it would appear at first. Be sure to obtain a list of sizes from your missionary. If you make clothing for children, remember that they grow! Make something for them to grow into. Perhaps you would rather donate a day a month apart from your regularly scheduled meeting for this special clothing project. Knitted and crocheted items are useful too.

MEDICINES

If your missionary is in medical work, why not collect sample medicines from your family doctor, local pharmacies, or pharmaceutical companies? Usually it is not difficult to gather several samples of pills and potions. Finding out what you have gathered and making some order from them will be a bit more taxing. It is best to have a doctor, nurse, or pharmacist available to discard dangerous drugs and make sure useable ones are properly marked with their generic or trade name, name of company, administration, usages, and side effects. Discard items which must be kept refrigerated. If you have a large quantity of several types, put them in separate double plastic bags or large bottles. (Many samples come wrapped in paper or light cardboard.) Medicine bottles or small containers can always be used on the field. But if there are only four pills of any one kind, don't bother sending them! A small dose of any type of medication is impractical and useless. Be sure you send sample medicines only with the blessing of your missionary, and direct them only to a knowledgeable, medically trained worker.

TRADING STAMPS AND COUPONS

If you have enough trading stamps, you can exchange them

for just about anything money will buy. When an entire congregation willingly donates its stamps, your missionary will be able to trade them for equipment and personal items. Coupons from cake mixes and other packaged goods can be redeemed (plus a small cost) for stainless steel, dinnerware, children's toys, and other items which you can, in turn, donate to missions.

CANCELLED POSTAGE STAMPS

Large stamp companies are in the market for used postage stamps. Check first with the company to see what types of stamps they are willing to buy (usually commemoratives and foreign stamps in mint or cancelled condition). Use the funds received to help in your missionary support. Be sure to instruct those involved in this project how to cut stamps off envelopes properly. In some situations, the missionary is able to sell our stamps overseas for more than we can get here. So, ask first which he would prefer, the money or the stamps.

WORK PROJECTS

Attention men and young people! This is for you. At a dollar per car, you can surely provide something for your missionary from a day of hard work. Young people may also plan a day to mow lawns, rake leaves, walk dogs, or tend gardens, in order to raise money for a necessary item.

These projects listed only scratch the surface of what you can provide for your missionary. You will be able to add dozens more which may fit your budget, congregation, and missionaries, far better than any of these.

11

MISSIONARY PRAYER LETTERS

Among the many responsibilities missionaries face is the matter of keeping in touch with friends, churches, prayer partners, and financial supporters in the States. Needless to say, this is a time-consuming and expensive project, if the missionary has several interested friends. A list might include from four hundred to twelve hundred names.

In the ideal situation, your missionary can have his letter prepared on the field and sent under foreign postage. Because of censorship, cost, or time factors, this is usually impractical, perhaps impossible. This, then, is where you can step in. Although you may wish to take it on as an individual project, it will be far less of a burden in the end if a group or class within the church is willing to assume this responsibility. It will take a few hours apart from your scheduled class sessions, but it will give you a wonderful opportunity to get to know one another better, work on a vital project, and become involved in missions in a practical way.

One member of the group should be appointed secretary. This one will correspond with your missionary, maintaining a supply of praise and prayer requests to share with the entire group. This will bring about a personal interest in his work and ministry and will produce a feeling of "family" interest. The secretary will also receive the original copy of each prayer letter after arranging a working schedule with the missionary concerning how many letters will be sent each year and the

approximate dates they will be sent. Planning in advance
will help the group considerably.

After the original letter arrives, the group can gather for
action. Some will be responsible for writing the final form of
the letter. With the prior consent of the missionary, rewording
or rewriting may be necessary. The facts should be maintained,
but it is possible that the format can be made more
readable, the grammar improved, the length made more satisfactory,
or the verbs made more active. Some in the group
may be especially skilled in the art of editing.

Someone may be able to provide sketches or line drawings
for the letter. Or perhaps the missionary would be willing
to send a good number of short items which could be produced
into a one- or two-page "newspaper." Pictures sent by
your missionary can be utilized with various titles and art-
work supplied by the group.

Several people should be appointed to maintain an updated
address list. After each mailing, approximately 10%
of the letters on an average list will be returned for a corrected
address. Others will notify you of such a change. Not
only does the master list need to be corrected and additions
and deletions made, but your missionary must also receive
a list of these changes to keep his own mailing list current.

After the final draft has been readied, someone types a
stencil which is then run off on a duplicating machine. If the
work is to be done by a professional printer, someone must be
responsible to see that the material reaches him, that he understands
exactly what he is to do, and someone must be responsible
to receive the finished product.

Meanwhile, with the corrected address list at hand, several
people can work on purchasing and addressing envelopes.
These can be typed, printed, or handwritten, but must be
neat, legible, and include a zip code.

Other folks will be engaged in applying return address

stickers or using a rubber return address stamp which includes the notation, "Return Postage Guaranteed."

If no folding machine is available, the letters will have to be processed by hand so they will fit in the envelopes properly. Some from the group will stuff envelopes. Others can seal them. Still others will stamp them. If you send the letters by first class mail, commemorative stamps make the envelopes look more attractive than ordinary postage or metered mail. You may, however, wish to obtain a postage permit allowing you to send the letters at a reduced rate.

The final procedure in the prayer letter process is to assign one or more individuals to place the letters in the mail.

As you work together, you come to know each other better; you become better acquainted with your missionary and gain a more personal interest in him; you can help provide the cost of sending the letters; you can ease a burden; you will have a part in missionary work, and God will reward you for this important ministry.

No one is excluded from this privilege. If your group is large, take on the work of several missionary letters. If it is small, provide this service for one. Above all else, do it as unto the Lord. Attractive prayer letters are a vital part of a missionary's responsibility. And you can be an important link in his chain of communication.

12

HOW TO MAKE CHILDREN AWARE OF MISSIONS AND MISSIONARIES

The church has too often neglected teaching children that essential and vital element of missions. In some cases, we thought it enough to teach youngsters, "God is love" and "Jesus saves." Our priority has been placed upon John 3:16 and Revelation 3:20. And it is right that we should be concerned about our children's salvation. But too long we have stressed this one doctrine to the neglect of the child's spiritual growth in discipleship, whether he is of nursery age or in his teens. We have not conveyed to him the full scope of Christianity. We have not challenged him as we should with the work and witness of God's servants worldwide. We have not given him a proper opportunity to serve the Lord and become involved in a ministry which befits his own particular talents and needs. We have not allowed him to look at missions with a view to offering himself to the Lord for this type of work.

A child is never too young to become involved in the missionary program of the church. It can be an enlightening and educational process for him. But it should be far more than putting pennies in a missionary bank or praying, "God bless Mr. Smith in Africa," albeit, these two ministries are essential.

The youngest child loves to hear stories. Tell him missionary tales. Records of missionary stories are available. Flannelgraph stories are effective, and most mission fields are now represented in this way. Flash-card mission stories can also be found at your local Christian bookstore. Children love to color. Use missionary pictures.

Children are intrigued by anything they can touch or handle. Curios and artifacts from other countries or cultures will fascinate them. Try taking a paper bag to class each week or once each month with a single object in it. Explain the object and the place from which it came. Let the children handle it and ask questions. Some items may be too fragile to pass around. These can be put in a place where all can see them and be able to talk about them, even though they cannot actually feel these items.

As the child becomes older, he will be interested in the countries where your missionary serves. He will begin to appreciate listening to tapes sent from the field, especially if the missionary is kind enough to include several familiar sounds of his country and to explain them, and to let his children talk too.

Missionary songs and memory verses should be included as a regular part of the worship service. Many churches find that designating a particular Sunday each month as missions Sunday has proven effective.

Even primary and junior children will enter into a quiz session based on their knowledge of their missionaries, their mission boards, their type of work, and where they are located.

Older children should be assigned projects periodically, and among these should be reports on missionary biographies, excerpts from missionary newsletters or a synopsis of the life, family, and work of one of your church missionaries.

The prayer support of children is of utmost value to your missionaries. A child *fully* believes what many of us *say* we believe—that God can do anything we ask or think. A child is not afraid to ask God to do the impossible. He just figures God will do it because He says He will. And much to the surprise of many sophisticated adults, God *does* do it! Never despise the words of a child's prayer.

Keep children informed of missionary prayer requests. You might consider putting the requests on slips of paper, having the children draw out one request each week and pray for that need before the group. Each one would then take the slip home and pray during that week for that individual, board, or project.

Be sure to ask your missionaries to visit or speak to your Sunday school department when they are available. Make sure there is an opportunity for the children to ask questions.

Perhaps you have foreign students living or studying in your area. Give them an opportunity to speak to your children and to tell them what life is like in their country. You may even wish to give those of a different religious background an opportunity to speak. It is essential that children become aware of the fact that Christianity is not the only belief which has intelligent followers. We have tried to shelter our children from these outside contacts. But what better way can they learn the truth of the gospel message than to become acquainted with other beliefs and compare them under the guidance of a dedicated spiritual counselor? They will find for themselves the assurance and reality of the Christian walk, and are less likely to be drawn away later by a persuasive person of an erroneous faith. This is especially true with junior and senior high young people.

Entertaining missionaries in your home gives your children a splendid opportunity to discover who a missionary is and what he does. It helps "dethrone" these workers and make them human. Your children will come to understand that these servants are down-to-earth, educated, people-oriented individuals. And surprise, surprise! They will learn that not all missionaries are women! The boys in your family will appreciate the fact that men are serving God and enjoying it!

Encourage your children to correspond with missionary children on the field. This type of pen-pal communication can benefit both the missionary's children and your own.

Of course, one of the best ways to involve your children in missions is to allow them to take an active role in outreach and witness. Many people have been won to Christ because a child decided to play church, set up an orange-crate pulpit in his back yard, and "taught" a lesson to his buddy Joe, old Grandpa Smith, and anyone else around.

Young people may form Reach-Out groups to hand out tracts, take a community religious census, speak on street corners (with permission from the proper authorities), or provide programs at hospitals, nursing or convalescent homes, and retirement centers. They may be allowed the privilege of witnessing at a nearby rescue mission. Budding musicians should be utilized in church services and for other ministries both within and outside of the church. Special prayer groups may be formed to remember missions specifically. Involvement with those who work in coffeehouses, home Bible classes for children, after-school Bible studies, open-air ministries, and other forms of Christian service will allow these young folk to begin to have a feeling for missionary endeavor.

Younger children can make scrapbooks for an Indian hospital, color pictures for use in teaching in a mission church, or make their own original invitations which the pastor may wish to leave at homes he visits. An invitation created by a child is read and often heeded. This is real missionary work!

As young people come to the age when they are deciding what their lifework should be, the consideration of missionary work ought to be a very natural thing. After all, it provides challenges and satisfactions that are found in any other job one could choose, far more than many. Although financial remuneration cannot be considered equitable for such a painstaking ministry, the joys of missionary service can never be measured in dollars and cents. No work can satisfy merely because of the money it provides.

Allowing your children to become acquainted firsthand

with missions and missionaries is one of the greatest privileges you can afford them.

Planning a youth missionary conference to coincide with your adult annual conference will produce excellent results also.

In conclusion, involve your children in missionary activities; don't be afraid God may call them to the ends of the earth; and don't neglect one of the most emphasized themes of the entire Word of God—that of missions. Give children and young people an opportunity to give their resources and their selves for the cause of Christ. Teach them well, for they will be tomorrow's leaders in the church and in the world. The impetus of missions really rests with them—and *you*.

13

THE MISSIONARY ROOM

Most of us do not realize what it is like to come "home" for a three- to twelve-month stay with little more than a couple of suitcases for each member of the family, no household equipment, and no resources to go out to clothe the family and furnish a home or apartment. It is frustrating to your missionary, but this is the situation in which he often finds himself. When he leaves for the field, he usually takes enough supplies to last the term, but at the end of that time, he may be threadbare and out of fashion.

"But," you may say, "my missionary always appears on the platform looking well dressed." Was he there for only a meeting or a day? If he was there for a week of conference, how many changes of suits did you notice? You see, most missionaries have one special item in their wardrobe. It is used only for weddings and funerals on the field, and it is their Sunday best upon their return to the States!

Then, unless he is housed at a missionary furlough home, which is completely furnished (including a well-stocked refrigerator upon his arrival), or lives with friends or relatives, he is not prepared with dishes, pots and pans, towels, linens, dry mop, broom, or garbage pail.

What if your missionary does not have such a well-provided situation? What can you do? You *can* be a resource person and tell your missionary whom to contact at Good Will Industries, the Salvation Army, or the corner bargain basement resale outlet. Think, though, how much better it would be for your church to take on a missionary room as a project worthy of its support.

Many churches already have such a program in existence. A room in the church may be designated, or one of the families in the congregation may be willing to offer a room or the basement of their home. This is a permanent project and requires a good amount of time and work. As it grows and interest is stimulated, more space will be needed, so plan for expansion from the beginning.

The idea of the missionary room is to keep it stocked with just about anything you can think of which you use in your daily routine: clothing, food, household goods, furniture, linens, toys, pencils, pens, crayons, writing paper, dishcloths, jewelry, hair rollers, scarves, shoestrings, skates, boots, raincoats, purses, umbrellas. Name it, and it has a good use if it is in good condition. The whole congregation should be made aware of the fact that such a room is now available for donations. Perhaps a fairly detailed list could be formulated by the women's missionary society or the church mission board. This could be distributed by mail, inserted in the church bulletin, or given to each person as he leaves the church on a specified Sunday. One list should be posted permanently on a centrally located bulletin board. Short announcements should be made from the pulpit and in the bulletin periodically, and reports should be given as to the status of the room and special items which may be needed for specific individuals.

An amazing number of items lie in our closets, attic, garage, or basement that are of no use to us, but that could provide a basic necessity for someone else. Perhaps you have redecorated a room in your home and have purchased new furniture to fit the new decor. Donate your used but useful furniture to the missionary room. Perhaps you were recently married, and when you combined your belongings with those of your spouse, you found you really had far too many dishes, an extra TV or radio, or duplicated gifts. Or you may have gone on a diet and have had to purchase a new wardrobe. (Some may have gone in the other direction, too!) Your clothes are in fashion, almost new, but they just do not fit. Remember that pair of shoes that pinch? The soles don't have a mark on them. Remember the doll you bought Sandi and she never played with? Remember the shirt that Jon outgrew before he had worn it twice? And what about the trading stamps and coupons that you have collected for no particular reason, except you hate to throw things away? And those sale items you bought because they were such a bargain, but you will never use (the pack of twelve lightbulbs or sponges, the shampoo with the free styling comb, the pink toilet tissue which doesn't match your blue bathroom, a singing teakettle, etc.).

For the moment, however, simply stop and think of those items you have that you would never miss. Jot them down on a piece of paper. Don't list any item which is not in good condition. The best way to determine the usefulness of an item is to ask yourself the question, "If I didn't have one, would this be acceptable for my own use?" If you would be ashamed or embarrassed with it, throw it out: don't give it to the missionary room. A Teflon frying pan without its Teflon is not a good bargain!

Once you have your list (and don't forget those tools and garden implements in the garage), submit it to the person in charge of the missionary room. List the condition of the items, the dimensions of furniture, the sizes of dresses, shoes, boots, suits, and so on. He will carefully review the list and request any or all of the things you have listed. (If you have a place to store the furniture, he may ask that you keep it until it is needed.) The rest can be placed in the missionary room.

When your missionary is planning to visit your church, he should be told of this special room. A time should be scheduled for him to view the items available, and he should be allowed to take anything he needs, as much as is useful to him. Some may not need much. Others may be planning to make their headquarters too far away to make it practical to take furniture with them from your supply. But others will consider the room a gold mine—clothes for the entire family, dishes, flatware, pots, pans, linens—and with what gratitude they will accept the things you have provided.

In many instances, after the furlough months are over, the missionary will return household goods which are still in decent condition so they can be used by other families who will need them. But in no case should the missionary feel obligated to return anything which has been given to him.

The director of this project and his assigned helpers should make sure that the room is kept tidy at all times. It should resemble a tiny department store, not a junk room. Items of clothing should have their sizes clearly marked. (In some cases, the size will no longer be visible in store-bought articles, and if they have been made at home, there will be no size. Thus it is very important to get that listing from the donor and mark all items as soon as they are processed.) Clothes and shoe racks should be set up according to size. Sheets and pillowcases should be carefully arranged according to twin, single, double, or king size. Games should be checked to see that all parts are included. Boxes which are split at the corners must be taped securely. Books should be arranged according to categories.

Even when extreme care is taken, some things will have to be discarded. People donate unsuitable items in spite of all requests for useful donations.

Your missionary room should never be allowed to become a place where well-worn, unwanted, and scrubby articles are deposited at random. It should be a highlight of your missionary interest, kept in order, and used often.

In churches which do not support a large number of overseas missionaries, such a room may still provide a missionary outreach in the community. There are often those who because of fire, loss of job, illness in the family, or natural disasters need the items which you could supply through such a ministry. Rescue missions, classes in the ghettos, orphanages, Indian work—home missionary work of all types and descriptions—is carried out in your state or your city. Your room could be a blessing and help to these workers as well as to those to whom they minister.

As stated earlier, your missionary room project will take time and hard work. But it is a simple and practical way to provide for others. It is even possible to receive income tax credit for your donations under certain conditions. Check with your local Internal Revenue Service office concerning this.

If your missionary will not be visiting you immediately upon his return from the field and he is headquartered some distance from you, write to him telling what things you have available and ask if he needs any of them. If clothing is available, ask him to specify his family's sizes. At his request, pick out a number of items, box them, and send them to his home. If someone in the church knows him personally, let that one help pick out items which seem right for him.

Just a reminder: If supplies get low in any category, a special announcement in the church bulletin, local newspaper, or from the pulpit should bring in the needed goods.

14

EMPHASIZING MISSIONS THROUGH-
OUT THE CHURCH

If the missions program is to grow and attract others to join its ranks, it must be kept in the forefront of the church calendar, emphasized sufficiently, and reports shared periodically. There are many ways of doing this. Let's mention just a few of them.

MISSIONARY MAP

A world or area map should be posted conspicuously in the church. Flashing or colored lights in the places where your missionaries serve can be wired up. Perhaps pictures of those who serve may be placed in their area of service, or as a border, with ribbons tacked between the picture and the area of service. (Pictures should be brought up-to-date at least once every two years.)

POSTERS

Effective display posters can be made by placing the following material on colored poster board: your missionary's picture, his mission board, his area of service, his type of ministry, his field address, and the amount of money committed to him by the congregation. A picture which shows him at his work on the field is most effective.

TAPES

Ask your missionary to send a five- or ten-minute tape, telling of his work and including sounds that would be of interest to the folks in the States (Muslim prayer call, children singing, camel bells, donkeys braying, etc.).

SLIDES

Perhaps slides can be sent with a short taped description from your missionary, or a written description may be included. Be sure to view slides before showing them to the church. If you support a mission board or Christian organization, they are very apt to have slide-tape presentations you may borrow at little or no cost. If your church supports several missionaries, be sure to obtain a slide of each individual or family. Keep your file updated. At least once every three months, project these slides at a midweek service. Keep the congregation mindful of the missionary, his field of service, and his type of ministry.

SUNDAY BULLETIN

Each week, be sure you place the name of one or two of your church missionaries with their current address (even when on furlough) in the church bulletin. This will remind people to pray for and write to these workers.

SPECIAL PRAYER

During each Sunday morning service, an individual should be chosen to pray for the specific needs of one or two of the church missionaries. It is good to pray for those listed in the bulletin, unless emergency requests have been received concerning specific individuals.

MISSIONARY BOOKLETS

The missionary committee, a group within the church, a Sunday school class, or an individual may be willing to work on putting together a mimeographed booklet to inform the congregation about your missionaries. Information should include the names of all members of the family (including ages of the children), birthdays, and anniversaries; the area, country, and continent of service should be stated along with the mission board under which each one serves. General prayer requests should be given. These booklets will need to be brought up to date annually. Don't forget to give a description of boards, projects, and organizations which receive funds from your total missionary contributions. Such booklets may be distributed to each church member, or be left at the church to be used as a guide for prayer meetings, so that individuals can pray for a family or organization more intelligently.

SPEAKERS

Avail yourself of missionary speakers in your area, and be sure to give special invitations to your own church missionaries to visit and speak during their furlough. Organizations and mission boards are always happy to provide representatives to speak whenever you request them.

FILMS

Many mission boards have excellent missionary films available. Utilize these 16-mm sound, color presentations at your midweek service, youth meeting, missionary conference, evening service, or for special occasions. Ask the boards under which your missionaries serve to inform you if and when they have a new film available on their fields of service.

AIR LETTER FORMS

Each week, have one of your missionary committee members address six air forms to each of the missionaries prayed for and mentioned in the weekly bulletin. Put these forms in a designated spot in the church and allow them to be taken by anyone who is serious about writing to these folks. Be sure to have your pastor announce their availability and where they are located.

MUSIC

Missionary music should be included in the regular services of the church. A missionary cantata produced by the choir will emphasize your program in a beautiful, challenging and expressive way.

MISSIONARY MEETINGS

Many churches have women's missionary meetings and prayer groups, but the work of missions is not the responsibility of women only. Why not have a men's missionary prayer group, perhaps meeting for breakfast once a week or once a month? Or a men's fellowship which includes missions in its program?

NEWS LETTERS

Missionary prayer letters are distributed in order to allow the folks at home the privilege of sharing joys and sorrows, answers to prayer and requests for it. These letters should be shared with the entire church family by putting excerpts on a bulletin insert, or by a synopsis at services. (If your church supports just one or two missionaries, the entire letter should be shared.)

GIVING GRAPH

There should be visual means for the congregation to see what progress they are making toward meeting their missionary budget.

MISSIONARY DISPLAY

A table, wall, glass-encased bulletin board, or cabinet should display items relevant to your missionaries. This should be rearranged regularly. The time element will be determined mainly by the number of missionaries your church supports. A picture of your missionary with his name clearly stated, along with his mission board and field of service should be prominently displayed. Curios, flag of the country, map of the area, pictures, sample of his language, a personal letter to the congregation (one page only), and other items may be added to the display. If items can be removed easily (stamps, coins, artifacts) be sure a responsible person is placed in the area to keep items from becoming "lost" or broken.

BULLETIN BOARDS

Make your bulletin boards most effective by changing them often and include notes, clippings, and items of interest about your missionaries and their countries in your format.

FOOD FROM AFAR

At your next covered-dish supper, women's meeting, or father-son banquet, serve foods from other countries. Recipes are easily obtained, and meals are no more difficult to prepare than American dishes. Ever try spaghetti, or chili, or chop suey? In large cities, catered meals of French, Italian, Mexican, Japanese, or Chinese food are easily obtained. In small towns, the ladies will enjoy creating chicken *pulao,* or spare ribs and sauerkraut with hot potato salad. If you don't know what your missionary eats, write and ask him.

PLACE MATS

Some mission boards have place mats available to advertise their work. If the board you support does not, it might be possible to have mats printed with a map of the world and the names of your missionaries in their areas of service. These, then, can be used whenever food is served at the church.

MISSIONARY CONFERENCE

In many churches, this is the hub around which the church wheel moves. If it is well-planned and advertised, it will produce tremendous attention, participation, and response. No matter how important and successful this endeavor, its impact must be carried throughout the year by keeping the congregation exposed to missionaries and their activities.

All of these activities are part of our total involvement in missionary support. As Peter Marshall once said, "Small deeds done are better than great deeds planned."

15

HOW TO SUPPORT ACCEPTED CANDIDATES

An accepted missionary candidate has entered a no-man's-land, where he is neither fish nor fowl, layman nor missionary. He is in the throes of great adjustments, as he moves forward into what will soon become his sphere of influence. He is something like a young bird that has just been pushed out of his nest by his mother. Hopefully, he will learn to stay aloft.

You can support a candidate by giving him confidence, and the first move in this direction is to allow him access to your church and to your home.

Most churches that have any interest in missions are anxious to obtain missionary speakers for their services. Fewer are happy about allowing a "green" candidate to take over. After all, he has no firsthand experience in his field, he cannot attest to his living and working situation, he has no lurid stories to tell of the hardships and privations of the people; and if he has slides, they have been borrowed and are as foreign to him as they are to his audience. His ability to answer questions is hindered because of his lack of field experience.

Remember, however, that he does have a Christian testimony! He can share God's leading in his life. He can express his hopes, aspirations, and goals for his term of service; and, after all, how does one become a missionary if he is not first an accepted candidate?

Make the candidate feel wanted and necessary to the entire missionary cause. Allow him to become acquainted with you and assure him of your continuing interest after he leaves your area. Ask friends in other groups if they would like to have the candidate speak to them. He probably needs additional contacts for prayer and financial concern. Invite him to work in your vacation Bible school, at your youth camp, with your Sunday school, or to assist the pastor with visitation and follow-up work. Even if you cannot make a financial commitment to the candidate, you can befriend him. He needs this as much as anything else. Be enthusiastic about the work he will be doing. Let him know you will be with him in spirit at all times.

Allow him to be himself. Don't force him to be someone or something he is not. Don't expect him to act like a mature and seasoned missionary statesman. He may become that, but at present he is an untried servant offering himself to the Lord for missionary service.

The candidate may not be able to answer all your questions, but asking them may help him to become better acquainted with the world he is about to enter as he does research to answer you.

You may be able to help him with his presentation. Perhaps you have visited the country he will be serving in. You may have learned things that he has not yet encountered, such as experiences with culture shock. Share with him what you know to help him to grow. If he seems too idealistic, don't disparage his zeal and commitment.

He might welcome suggestions regarding what you would like to hear about in his newsletters. You might have the talent required to help him design his prayer card, or you may be able to provide the finished product for him.

If and when you decide to carry some of the financial support of a candidate, don't wait until he leaves for the field to start your giving. Start right away. All funds given to his account will accrue toward outgoing expenses (equipment, travel, language school). He also must have living expenses while involved in his deputation ministry.

Providing equipment for the first-term missionary is a joyous privilege, perhaps even more so than for returning missionaries. Ask for a list of needed items. Perhaps you or your group can provide some of these things. The supply of these items is as necessary as his monthly support.

If you know of stores or dealers who offer a discount to religious workers, tell the candidate about them. It may be possible for him to obtain certain necessary items of equipment at a sizeable discount through your contacts. This, of course, would certainly be to his advantage. Share with him your acquaintance with such organizations and stores.

If a candidate must attend language school in an area other than his field of service, he may not be able to take all of his worldly goods with him, nor can they be shipped to his field before his arrival. You may be able to do him a great service by offering to lock his pieces of equipment (barrels, footlockers, boxes), provide storage space for them until he requests that they be sent, and then send them at the designated time. If you are uncertain as to the actual procedure required for shipping, contact the home office of the candidate's mission board. They will be happy to give you easy instructions.

Moral support is a necessary item the candidate may not think to put on a list of needs. Be very cautious about remarks made to singles, because you may not know something important. Something said in fun about finding a mate may hurt the person and cause bad feelings. Suggesting that he will soon find happiness in marriage on the field may not be the best therapy for a heartbroken, dedicated worker who has tried to put his devotion to Christ above his love for a sweetheart. If you don't know the person well, you are wiser to not refer at all to his single state.

It does little good to mention to married couples with young children the dangers they are bringing upon their family by going into the bush. There is no safer place than the center of God's will. The candidates have faced this issue and have concluded that they are as safe in snake-infested swamps as they are crossing the main street in their hometown. God will not forsake them. Psalm 139 is their strong tower and fortress. Your doubts should not be allowed to cast doubt upon their desire to serve in a difficult situation. Remember too that many missionaries serve in areas and conditions not unlike those in the homeland.

If you are near enough to do so, be present when your candidate leaves the homeland for his field of service. Perhaps you can plan your vacation in such a way that you can be at the dock or airport at the time of departure. This added personal interest will be greatly appreciated by the candidate, and will help you to understand a bit more of the joys and struggles which a candidate experiences as he embarks upon his work as a missionary.

Pray for him as he spends those hours on the plane. For even though he left the homeland as an accepted missionary candidate, he will arrive at his destination as a new missionary. It will suddenly dawn upon him that he is not sufficient for the task. Your prayers will help him to get things into focus and realize that His sufficiency is entirely of God. And you have a share in it by being a colaborer together with Him in the great ministry of reaching people for Jesus Christ.

16

PERSONAL INVOLVEMENT IN MISSIONS

Somewhere along the line, we have confused our concept of missionary work with the mistaken notion that the mission field is "out there," and God chooses only a few to take part in this endeavor. Too long we have put our check in the church offering, prayed "God bless the missionaries," and considered our responsibility cared for.

Nowhere in the Word of God do we find that the mission field is afar off. One of the reasons Christianity has had so little influence in our day is our lack of personal involvement in serving the Lord. You see, every individual is either a missionary or a mission field. Therefore, the "mission field" may be your own household, your own family, and, surely, your own neighborhood. Why is it that we are willing to pay others to do this type of work and we are so unwilling to do it ourselves?

"But God didn't call me to do it," you plead. And I say, "Poor excuse." God has given general instructions to all of us. "Ye shall be my witnesses." "Go and teach." "Go and tell." "Go ye into *all* the world and preach." "Ye are the salt of the earth." One cannot read far in His Word before he finds that sharing the good news ought to be as natural as breathing. We are commanded to gossip the gospel.

If you are to support missionaries who *do* serve "out there," you will be better able to enter into their labors and understand some of their problems if you have become a missionary yourself. It is easy to be judgmental and critical of the Lord's servants when we look on from the outside. Instead, we should be like the wise old Indian who said, "Let me not judge my brother until I have walked two moons in his moccasins."

Start a neighborhood Bible class in your home; volunteer for visitation in homes in the community; distribute tracts on a street corner, on the bus, plane, or train; become involved in hospital or convalescent home visitation; witness at the local rescue mission; teach a Sunday school class; be a sponsor for a young people's group; become a camp counselor; work in a coffeehouse; do personal work at an evangelistic meeting; use your musical abilities as a means of witness; teach a children's class in your home, garage, or back yard; invite a foreign student over for dinner next Sunday; share Jesus Christ with your friends and business associates face to face; write letters to friends to whom you cannot witness personally; always be ready to give a reason for the hope that is within you.

Look over this list—and there are many other ministries which could have been added—and your response will undoubtedly be, "I just don't have the time (or the training, or the ability) ," or, "I'm basically shy, and I find it impossible to speak to others about salvation."

Perhaps you are already engaged in one of these avenues of witness and you cannot take on another responsibility because of your full-time job and the preparation time required for your ministry. Everyone would agree that it is far better to do one thing well than to do many things in a careless and slipshod manner.

Yet think for a moment. When we think of our missionary "out there," don't we think of him as a jack-of-all-trades? A servant of the people twenty-four hours each day? We expect that he will spend *all* his time ministering to the people, teaching the Bible, preaching the gospel. We picture him

as a constant, steady stream of endless good cheer and in-
defatigable zeal. We allow him no time for rest, recreation,
vacation, family fun times, preparation, sickness, or sightsee-
ing. We think of him as being deeply involved in every endeavor known to Christians. Somehow we picture him as
pilot, doctor, teacher, pastor, secretary, photographer, preacher, musician, counselor, writer, and fix-it man. Yet the truth
is, he cannot do *every*thing. He will never be able to reach
all the twenty million souls to whom he has been sent. We
imagine him as being the great white father, accepted by all as
the bearer of truth. We see the streets lined with hordes of
people waiting for his arrival. We think the nationals are at
a loss when he departs for another area of service or comes
home for furlough. We feel he must be a giant of the faith
with spiritually, mentally, emotionally, and physically satisfying answers to his own and others' questions. He is bold
and unwavering in his love for God. He is a friend to everyone and loved by all who come in contact with him. He de-
lights in the heaven-like fellowship with his fellow workers.
Except for the snakes and lions he encounters daily, little
else crosses his path to upset him. His children are models of
perfection. His wife fully understands him. Life is a lark,
and he never regrets for a second that he decided to be a missionary! Now truthfully, have you ever pictured missionaries
something like this?

It is not possible for us to walk in our missionary's moccasins. Most of us will not even have an opportunity to visit
the field to see, hear, feel, and smell it for ourselves. But if
we have become personally active in a ministry at home, we
will better understand the kind of support our missionary
needs.

The first thing you will realize is that witnessing is not as
easy as some of our personal evangelism books would try to
tell us. We are treading on Satan's toes, and he begins to

make it difficult for us. And he is no less interested in your missionary's work than he is in yours.

The next thing we discover is that people are not filling up our homes, Sunday school rooms, auditoriums, churches, offices, or any other place waiting to hear the gospel. Very few are spontaneously interested in "being preached at." People are content with the status quo, whether they are atheists, agnostics, or heathen of any type and description. They are, unfortunately, quite unwilling to give up their traditional beliefs simply because some stranger or acquaintance tells them there is a better way—the *only* way. Do *you* believe everything you hear? Others don't either. Our missionary too finds that most of the people around him are content in their own religion, if, indeed, they have any form of faith.

Not all missionaries are outgoing individuals. Button-holing and collaring folks in order to push the gospel down their throats is just not their way of doing things. And not every sentence which proceeds from their tongue has a scriptural context. Indeed, in many lands, it takes months of idle chatter before the gospel can be mentioned. Winning friends takes time. Once they are won, the gospel can be more freely shared.

If you witness to people yourself, you will understand the frustration your missionary faces when he longs to blurt out the good news of the gospel but must wait until the time is ripe. (I wonder if the Lord Jesus ever pleaded with the Father to allow Him to come to earth earlier than He did, because of His concern for mankind.) If you work with people at all, you will better understand your missionary's prayer request when he writes, "Pray that we might have opportunities to witness to this individual." It is not a simple matter of quoting John 3:16 and 1 Corinthians 15:3-4 and expecting the sinner to be convinced of Christ.

As you become more involved in your personal ministry,

you will begin to hear the doubts and questions that people
raise; you will see the reasons many choose to remain apart
from Christ; you learn what the world thinks of hypocritical
and powerless Christians; you experience the very real pres-
sures of satanic warfare; you can also rejoice when you see a
soul in darkness turn to the light and become converted.

You will not always agree with your co-workers. There
will be differences of personalities and opinions. There may
be envying and jealousy. Each individual thinks his way of
doing things is the *right* way, and some feel it is the *only* way.
And missionaries are no less human. Some of their biggest
problems "out there" come from the friction they generate
with co-workers.

Do you feel your missionary should always carry a Bible
and a handful of tracts to give to every person he meets? Do
you do this? When was the last time you gave a tract or
left one with anyone? "Oh," but you say, "that's a missionary's job. That's what he gets paid for."

So *that's* it! A missionary is obliged to witness because you
are helping to pay him to do so! Perhaps this accounts for the
lack of results we sometimes see. We are sitting around the
sides of the arena, watching the world pass out into a Christ-
less eternity, condemning young people whom we decide
should have offered themselves for missionary service, scratch-
ing our heads and wondering why our missionaries are not accomplishing more in their areas of service, and hoping no one
ever asks us to teach a Sunday school class, sing in the choir,
distribute tracts at the hospital, or attend the midweek prayer
service.

Don't we find it easier to go from door to door and say,
"We're doing a church survey, and I want to ask you a few
questions," than to knock on a door and announce, "I'm concerned about your relationship with God, and I feel com-
pelled to share some good news with you concerning this
matter." Witnessing is not something we do for money. We

all ought to be doing it because we have a love and personal concern for individuals.

Let's get this straight once and for all. All the money in the world will not save a single soul. Your financial help cannot be expected to turn a man from the power of Satan unto God. It is only the witness of the Holy Spirit, usually combined with the testimony of a Christian, which can cause spiritually blinded people to see the truth as it is revealed in the Word of God. Your financial investment in a minister of the gospel is necessary so that he does not have to spend forty hours a week working to earn his own living. He has at least those forty hours to bear a witness to the world. It is important that you invest in an individual whose motivation and goal is to proclaim to needy souls the message of salvation in Jesus Christ. But he cannot do this with only your financial support. He must have your prayer support also. If you have entered upon a means of personal witness in Christian outreach, you will begin to see the absolute necessity of prayer support. And you will begin to pray simply, "Dear Lord, give him patience, love, understanding, wisdom, discernment, enlightenment; keep him from succumbing to temptation, his bad temper, his critical thoughts, his unkind actions; help him to redeem the time, to care for his family, to exude Christ through his being as well as in his saying and doing." You will see your missionary as a human being who needs the same things in life that *you* do, including love, praise, enjoyment, financial independence, comforts, acceptance, protection, escape from pain, and popularity. He has a desire to save time, avoid effort, gratify appetites, satisfy curiosity, be like those whom he admires, receive attention, avoid trouble, and take advantage of opportunities. These human needs are a part of each one of us.

As we begin to understand some of these things more fully, we shall approach missions and missionaries in an entirely different frame of mind than ever before. Missionaries are not looking for your sympathy, but if you can empathize with them, you have come a tremendously long way along the path of involved missionary support.

Remember that to know the will of God is the greatest knowledge; to find the will of God is the greatest discovery; and to do the will of God is the greatest achievement.

17

SHORT TERM AND SUMMER WORKERS

Even though we may have determined to tithe financially, our churches have fallen short of giving a tithe of its young people to the service of God. Perhaps we are further on our way toward this goal than ever before because of the many college-age as well as older folks who are giving a kind of tithe of their life in missionary service. The rise of programs involving work for two or three months during the summer (or at another more convenient time of year) and the six-month to two-year short term of service have greatly increased the number of people participating in the missionary program of the church.

In almost every case, it is the responsibility of the volunteer to obtain sufficient funds to get him to the field, maintain himself while there, and bring himself home again. You may wish to have a financial part or prayer partnership with one who has pledged himself to such a ministry.

It is a joy to be able to contribute one's financial resources for the purpose of seeing that missionary work is carried on, but an even greater joy comes to those who are willing to step out by faith for a short period to fill a gap and meet a specific need in mission ranks. You can volunteer for almost any country of the world and go under the auspices of almost any missionary organization. No matter what your background and experience, there may be an opportunity for you to serve.

Can you paint, build, tune pianos, teach, cook, care for children? Would you be willing to become a houseparent? A secretary? An accountant? A bookkeeper? Have you had experience in broadcasting, script writing, photography, engineering, administration? Are you a doctor, nurse, pharmacist, lab technician, anesthetist? Would you be willing to pastor a church for English-speaking foreigners in the country where you would serve? Do you have specialized training that could be helpful if shared with others on the field? There is no end to the needs for workers in the service of Christ around the world.

It is no longer unusual to hear of a doctor taking a leave of absence from his practice in order to devote six months or a year to overseas ministry. A lady visiting a mission field finds that there is need for a hostess at the field headquarters. She stays on for several months to meet the need while the regular hostess is on furlough. A management company offers to provide leadership courses for missionaries on the field. These services are vital. They provide extensive outreach to worldwide missions.

It takes people like yourself to offer such ministries. Becoming a part of the missionary task force of the world can be compared with nothing else, even if it is but for a short time. It cannot be purchased with money; it is not obtained through good intentions or lack of action. It is yours for the taking. Why not consider this possibility? You may be a college freshman with a free summer. Or perhaps you have retired after forty years of hard work. Or you may be somewhere in the middle. Why not offer yourself to a mission board for a short time of service? Or you may wish to contact one of the organizations which specializes in discovering your qualifications to fit them to the need of a particular mission or area of work through its short-term program. Some workers are required for a matter of only two to three weeks in order to do one specific job.

If you become involved in a venture of this type, you will be a changed person. Upon your return to the homeland, you will feel some of that unspeakable concern that missionaries try to tell us about; you will have seen needy people who are still without the joy of the knowledge of Christ because we have not yet shared Him with them; you will know from personal experience the need for additional workers; you will have experienced some of the thrill of worshiping and walking with brothers and sisters in Christ of whom you were previously unaware and with whom you will be spending eternity! You may decide to give more of yourself and what you possess for the sake of the gospel of Christ.

18

EVALUATING

You have been supporting for several months or years a particular mission, missionary, Christian school, organization, church, or other religious cause. You have not increased or decreased the amount of your support. You have not given much thought to what your money has been accomplishing or how it has been used or distributed. Perhaps it is time to take an accounting and ask some questions.

If you support a missionary, have you stopped to consider any of the following?

What are his present financial needs? Has his overall support need increased? Decreased? Have some of his supporters had to discontinue giving? Has his board required more support? Has his family increased? Decreased? Have you asked him lately about his financial picture? Has your income increased to the extent that you could contribute a greater portion of his support?

Perhaps your missionary has mentioned the need for work-account funds to be used for a vehicle, needed furniture, fuel, training of a national, care of an orphan, tuition for his college-age child, equipment necessary to the proper functioning of his school, radio station, bookstore, or evangelistic ministries. If you have not been able to provide funds yourself, have you shared these needs with friends who might be interested? For example, a friend was visiting missionaries in Japan. When she returned to our home church, she told us

that one of the missionaries we supported was very tired physically, and she felt part of this was due to the fact that he had
to ride a bicycle to and from his work every day—a round trip
of about fifteen miles through crowded Tokyo. Several in
our church responded to the need, seen firsthand; two weeks
later, sufficient funds were provided for the purchase of a
new Toyota.

Not only should we be concerned financially for missionaries. Other facts are worthy of thought. For example, has
your missionary changed his doctrinal views since you started
to support him? Are his beliefs in basic agreement with yours?
Is he remaining true to basic scriptural doctrines, or has he
gone off on a tangent? Supporting one whose teachings are
opposed to your understanding of the Scriptures is incongru-
ous and lacks divine unction.

In your assessment, take into account the attitude displayed
by your missionary toward his calling and work. Some folks
lose their zeal for continuing in the ministry to which they
were called. Some will admit that they are not really happy
with being a missionary, but they are not willing to step aside
and seek another ministry, for they feel out of step with life in
the States. Thus, they continue to work hard and long with
a critical attitude and unhappy plans, which result in a nar-
rowed outlook and a shattered personality. It would be far
better to cease support for such an individual. Providing for
him to stay in a place where he no longer fills a need and allowing him the opportunity of poisoning co-workers (both
missionary and national) with his dissatisfaction does not do
justice to the cause of Christ.

Perhaps the foremost cause of missionaries losing the support of those in the homeland is their lack of concern and
sharing with supporters. As a financial partner, you become
a colaborer together with God and your missionary. If the
one whom you support responds with an attitude that gives
you the feeling that it is only what is expected of you, you

have every right to consider dropping his support. Missionaries fall into three categories: (1) those who are ungrateful and feel that your money designated for them is an obligation you must pay them; (2) those who are grateful for your money but could care less about you, and if you find you are unable to continue their support, they cut you off without further word; and (3) those who are extremely grateful for your support, who share their lives with you, and are interested in your life, your needs, your prayer requests. These folks have a sense of understanding if you can no longer offer financial assistance and they will still keep in touch with you.

Now it is true that all that we do, we do as unto the Lord. Every good gift comes from Him in the first place, and we are merely returning a portion to Him through support of His work. However, it makes little sense to continue to support a cause in which you have little interest, or a missionary who by his very actions acknowledges that your giving means little or nothing to him. What kind of work or worker do you want to continue to support?

You may discover that your missionary no longer feels he has a commitment to the Lord for His work. He may become exceedingly critical of his board, the country to which he is assigned, and the work in which he is engaged. If he can no longer wholeheartedly do the work to which he has been assigned, it is well to consider what Solomon said in Proverbs 10:26, "As vinegar to the teeth, and as smoke to the eyes, so is the sluggard to them that send him." Such a one is not worthy of your support.

Have you been aware of your missionary's physical, emotional, and mental condition? If you question his fitness for service, contact his board and get the facts. It is difficult to decide what should be done in such cases, but if there are serious problems involved, you are not helping by allowing that individual to remain at his post. Sometimes it is difficult even for a mission board to cope with this situation. But if support is not forthcoming, it is quite certain that the person will be required to make other plans, including (hopefully) good professional care for the problem (s).

In your evaluation, you might want to consider rather seriously where your missionary is located, what type of ministry he has, how many he is able to reach with the gospel, and what the results have been. There are always winning causes and losing battles. Throwing money into a cause which is already doomed to failure is a waste. Find out how many are involved in the area, the number that should be available to do the job right, national involvement, type of training and opportunities of service available to national believers.

If you are giving support to an organization, keep up with what is going on. As a contributor, you have a right to speak out on issues. Questions ought not to go unanswered. If you have reason to believe your money is not being used as designated, that the organization does not exercise good stewardship, if there is much financial waste and little spiritual result, you have every right to discontinue your help.

It might be well to evaluate your own habits too. Did you decide to support a missionary organization or project on the basis of an emotional appeal, and are you continuing that support out of nothing but a sense of responsibility to keep your promise? Do you have a real interest in what your funds are providing? Or has giving become merely a matter of writing a check at designated intervals? Have you kept in contact with what this board is providing or producing? Have you felt that tossing your tithe in the offering basket has exonerated you from any personal responsibility in sending the gospel around the globe—or the neighborhood? Has it turned into a conscience gift—an expiation for not offering to become physically involved in the work of God? Is your giving the best you can do? Is it done in a spirit of Christian love and cheerfulness? Do you do it for the sheer joy of doing it, or because you fear the condemnation of God or man if you don't?

As a church, have you evaluated your whole missionary program? Have you readjusted your outreach according to the gifts received, or have you challenged the congregation to give more? Have you given due emphasis to stewardship for the cause of missions? Have people been kept adequately informed concerning commitments, offerings, and expenditures? Have special needs been presented? Has sufficient opportunity been given for support to be pledged? Do you maintain a separate budget for missionary endeavor? Is it made clear what makes up a missionary offering and why missions are important? Does your pastor believe fully in missions? Are your missionaries prayed for personally at services and by people in your congregation? Have opportunities been given to provide anything other than financial support to your workers? Has provision been made for those who would be willing to work and witness in your own community through Christian outreach?

It is necessary to evaluate our giving to the work of the Lord as carefully as we evaluate funds committed to a business enterprise. What we give and to whom we give it will help to determine the effectiveness of our support.

Our money, time, and talents are entrusted to us by the Lord. It is our responsibility, in turn, to entrust them to those who will continue to multiply their usefulness and bring forth fruit to the praise of His eternal glory.

OTHER BOOKS BY MARJORIE A. COLLINS

MANUAL FOR ACCEPTED MISSIONARY CANDIDATES
William Carey Library
1705 N. Sierra Bonita Avenue
Pasadena, CA 91104
Second edition, 1978, 125 pp., paperback

A guide for candidates who need to plan for deputation meetings, prayer/newsletters, prayer cards, setting up displays, obtaining outfit and equipment, packing, legal, financial and medical matters . . . and so much more. Useful for both candidates and those who work with candidates. The book closes with a selected bibliography of helpful resources for the prospective missionary.

MANUAL FOR MISSIONARIES ON FURLOUGH
William Carey Library
1705 N. Sierra Bonita Avenue
Pasadena, CA 91104
Second printing, 1978, 151 pp., paperback

Although each of the 29 short chapters in this book gives helpful hints for those who are ready to leave the field for furlough, Chapter 7 is the most important. Through the scores of questions asked, a person is able to determine how effective his/her life and ministry is as an individual and as a Christian worker.

DEDICATION: WHAT IT'S ALL ABOUT
Bethany Fellowship, Inc.
6810 Auto Club Road
Minneapolis, MN 55438
Copyright 1976, 154 pp., paperback

What happens after a Christian makes an initial commitment to Jesus Christ? This book gives suggestions as to what should and can happen. A guide for pastors, missions committees, church leaders and those who have taken or are considering taking a step of commitment to the Savior and to His service.

This book *Who Cares About the Missionary* is being made available because its thoroughly practical value to enable Christians to be more helpful to missionaries.

The publisher of this book has also published the following books:

PRACTICAL HELP FOR
CHRISTIAN WORKERS

This book is in its 11th printing and has grown from 64 pp. (1948) to a present 344 pp. It contains some 80 topics, largely on church work. Topics are also included for missionaries, children's workers and evangelists. A number of chapters give practical suggestions regarding trades and hobbies. There are 32 pages of pertinent information on BUILDING CHURCHES. Other topics in this area are photography, first aid and gardening.

A main feature is a section on FILING AND INDEXING including a 12 page CLASSIFIED INDEX, specially designed for Christian workers. A REFERENCE section lists several hundred Christian organizations, books and periodicals indexed topically, alphabetically and in a classified order.

GOD CREATED

This book presents "a unique interpretation of Genesis 1:1-10." The term "sequential creation" is used to describe God's creation work. We expect to have it revised and reprinted soon (1982). Complementary copies of the first printing are available for those interested and who may wish to make comments.

CURRENT PRICES

Who Cares About the Missionary? $2.00
Practical Help for Christian Workers $3.00
        Add 50¢ toward postage for one book and 15¢ for each additional copy.

You may send for additional information and for special quantity discount rates.

Don Wardell
Box 325
WINONA LAKE, Ind. 46590